A Community of the Imagination:

Seóirse Bodley's Goethe Settings

A Community of the Imagination:
Seóirse Bodley's Goethe Settings

edited by Lorraine ByrneBodley

Carysfort Press

A Carysfort Press Book in association with Peter Lang
A Community of the Imagination: Seóirse Bodley's Goethe Settings
Edited by Lorraine ByrneBodley
First published in Ireland in 2013 as a paperback original by
Carysfort Press, 58 Woodfield, Scholarstown Road
Dublin 16, Ireland
ISBN 978-1-78997-084-5
©2013 Copyright remains with the authors
Typeset by Carysfort Press
Cover design by Brian O'Connor

This book is published with the financial assistance of
The Arts Council (An Chomhairle Ealaíon) Dublin, Ireland

CONTENTS

ACKNOWLEDGEMENTS

A project like this will necessarily come to rely on the help of many people in different fields of musical, literary and critical expertise. Assembling the list of those who have actively supported and encouraged my work is a special pleasure, making me realize, once again, how fortunate I am.

Progress on this book was greatly facilitated by the generous decision of the Research Office, NUI Maynooth, to award me a publication subvention; their generous support and encouragement of this apograph proved crucial to its preparation and progress. Grateful thanks are also due to Dr Attracta Halpin and the NUI Publications Committee for their generous publication subvention which supported Brian O' Connor's cover design, so beautifully rendered.

Many happy hours have been spent listening to and discussing these works. I realize how immensely privileged I am to have enjoyed private renditions of both cycles in our home and to have watched them come into existence. The memory of Seóirse singing and playing through each song is a pearl beyond price. Both cycles were commissioned for and received their first performances at the 'Goethe and Music' conferences which I organised in NUI Maynooth. I am indebted to Kathleen Tynan (soprano), Sam McElroy (baritone) and Dearbhla Collins (piano) for their premiere of *Mignon und der Harfner* at the conference, *Goethe: Musical Poet, Musical Catalyst*, on Friday, 26 March 2004. I owe a special debt of gratitude to Sylvia O'Brien (soprano), Imelda Drumm (mezzo-soprano), the Mornington Singers and their gifted conductor, Dr Orla Flanagan, all of whom premiered *Gretchen* with Seóirse at the conference, *Music in Goethes Faust: Goethes Faust in Music*, NUI Maynooth on 20 April 2012. Sylvia's sensitive rendering of Gretchen and Imelda's formidable musical presence as the Böser Geist, accompanied by Seóirse at the piano, brought an informed audience of Germanists and musicologists to their feet: it was one of those momentous performances which is relived many times in one's memory. My colleagues and friends, Prof. Florian Krobb, and Dr Wolfgang Marx, who were at the heart of that conference, deserve special thanks for their encouragement and support.

These song cycles, in which Seóirse Bodley, one of the most eminent contemporary Irish composers, engages with the poetry of Goethe, one of the finest minds in European literature, are fine examples of cultural dialogue between Ireland and Germany. The publication of this apograph has been planned to coincide with Ireland holding the EU Presidency during the first six months of 2013 and to mark Seóirse Bodley's 80th birthday in April this year. The score will be launched at a concert of both cycles performed by Sylvia O' Brien (soprano), Owen Gilhooly (baritone), Imelda Drumm (mezzo-soprano), and David Adams (piano) on 28 April 2013. Grateful acknowledgement is made to the chant ensemble directed by Ruaidhrí Ó Dálaigh and to my colleague, Dr John O'Keeffe, for his advice. To Gavin O'Sullivan who greatly enriches Dublin's musical life through his Hugh Lane Gallery Sundays at Noon series, I express my deepest appreciation. I warmly acknowledge the generosity of the German Embassy and in particular, Dr Eckhard Lübkemeier, German Ambassador to Ireland, who magnanimously supported this venture. I am also deeply grateful to Evonne Ferguson, Director of the Contemporary

Music Centre and her colleague, Jonathan Grimes, for their warm endorsement of Seoirse's 80ᵗʰ birthday concert and launch. I am particularly indebted to the warmth and generosity of John Buckley whose unwavering support of Seóirse's music and warm endorsement of this apograph proved pivotal.

I owe much to those boon companions and lifelong friends, who have accompanied me on this musicological path. I warmly acknowledge a very deep debt of gratitude to Professor Harry White, whose unfailing encouragement has helped me past those occasional times when energies flagged, and whose friendship is of inestimable importance. I owe a very special debt of gratitude to the immensely knowledgeable and very kind, Professor Susan Youens, for being an unstinting support and guide: I am incalculably indebted to her for her unique friendship and stellar example. Two dear friends, Professor Gerard Gillen and Dr Patrick Devine, have helped me immeasurably with their unfailing good humour and gentle encouragement; they have my love and gratitude for their enduring friendship. It is a pleasure to acknowledge in writing Professor Julian Horton's scholarly certitude and musical resource; at every musicological gathering he is always to the fore, a guarantor of the good cheer and good will that have made our scholarly collaboration such a happy experience. I owe the very existence of this book to Dan Farrelly, General Editor of Carysfort Press and dearest of friends, whose unwavering support has been inimitable. Dan exercised his razor-sharp acumen on this manuscript; the good-humoured assistance of all at Carysfort Press has been outstanding. For the opportunity to share this work with an audience of colleagues and friends, I thank Barbara Dignam. I also found welcome encouragement from Gareth Cox whose biography, *Seóirse Bodley,* has been revelatory; his first reaction to this apograph mattered greatly. My thanks to Patrick Zuk, who organized the first international conference on Irish music and musicians at the University of Durham in July 2010, at which I presented a paper on Seóirse's songs, and to Seamus de Barra, for his wisdom and acuity on that occasion.

Numerous colleagues, friends and anonymous individuals in lecture audiences in Ireland, the UK, Germany, and North America have challenged ideas and supplemented information about Goethe's Gretchen, Mignon and the Harper. The distinguished roster that follows is symbolic rather than exhaustive: given the passage of ten years since my first monograph on Schubert's settings of these texts appeared, it is impossible to remember all the interesting conversations I have had, all the email messages kindly sent after a lecture or paper, and all the suggestions and advice offered. Thanks, therefore, to Julian Horton (University College Dublin); Denise Neary (Royal Irish Academy of Music); Adrian Scahill, Paul Higgins and Niall Kinsella (NUI Maynooth); Graham Johnson (Guildhall School of Music and Drama); Richard Stokes and Ian Partridge (Royal Academy of Music, London); Crawford Howie (Schubert Institute UK); Amanda Glauert (Royal College of Music, London); Martin Swales (University of London); Alison Browner (Frankfurt); Aylish Kerrigan (Stuttgart); Claus Canisius (Heidelberg); Christiane Schumann (Deutsche Schubert Gesellschaft, Duisburg); Walther Dürr (University of Tübingen); Richard Kramer (City University of New York); Blake Howe (Louisiana State University); Deborah Stein (New England Conservatory); Lisa Feurzeig (Grand Valley State University); Juergen Thym (Eastman School of Music); Laura Tunbridge (University of Manchester); John Michael Cooper (Southwestern University, Texas); Thomas Bauman (Northwestern University); Sharon and Harald Krebs (University of Victoria); Kathryn Whitney (Victoria Conservatory of Music); Marjorie Hirsch (Williams College); Brian Black (University of Lethbridge). The author and publisher wish to thank Ashgate for their permission to develop some of the contextual detail in Lorraine Byrne Bodley, *Schubert's Goethe Settings* (Ashgate, 2003).

The painting, Mignon (1828), by Friedrich Wilhelm von Schadow (1788-1862) which graces the cover is courtesy of akg-images/Museum der bildenden Kunst, Leipzig; the images by Harry Clarke illustrate the Street and Prison scenes of Goethe's *Faust 1* (author's private library) and the photograph of the plaque which now commemorates Goethe's original inscription of 'Wandrers Nachtlied' on the wall of a hunting lodge is the author's own.

A great debt of gratitude is due to one of the score's dedicatees – Professor Nicholas Boyle (Schroeder Professor of German, Magdalene College Cambridge), to whom Seóirse dedicated the *Gretchen* cycle. The first volume of essays I edited, *Goethe and Schubert: Across the Divide* (2003) went out into the world with Nicholas's blessing. During the past ten years as I struggled to come to terms with the musical life of the poet he himself compassed in his own superb biography, *Goethe. The Poet and the* Age, I have drawn inspiration from the clarity and depth of Nicholas's writing on Goethe and benefited greatly from his endorsement of my own. On each of his four visits to Maynooth with his charming wife, Rosemary, we benefited immensely from Nicholas's lectures delivered, as they were, with great intellectual and oratorical verve, and all questions answered with forensic resource. We always left the hall with a new spring in our step and after each event enjoyed their warm-hearted friendship.

Mignon und der Harfner is dedicated to Rolf Stehle, Director of the Goethe-Institut Dublin (2006-2012), in faraway Malaysia with his wife, Verena, and two children. During their Dublin sojourn, Rolf offered unwavering support and understanding of my many musicological ventures. I will always remember his immense kindness to me and wish him and his family every happiness in this next stage of their lives in South-East Asia.

This apograph is a very special one for me in that my husband's artistic gifts have here enveloped both of our interests. Seóirse's first Goethe setting, 'Wandrers Nachtlied' – written almost ten years to the day on which this book will be launched – was composed for the launch of my first monograph, *Schubert's Goethe Settings* (2003); the setting captures so beautifully the stillness evoked in Goethe's poem and experienced on our memorable visit to Illmenau together. We discovered together the original painting of Mignon by Wilhelm Friedrich Schadow on one of our many visits to the Museum der bildenden Künste during my six-month stint as Visiting Professor at the University of Leipzig in 2010. Seóirse's ongoing interest in my work – as unfailing as it is unobtrusive – acts as an inspiration and a stimulus: my gratitude to him for his continued support, and for sharing space in our lives with Goethe and Schubert over many years, has no limits. My final acknowledgement is to my daughter, Bláthnaid, who patiently endured occasional absences necessitated by my work on this score and patiently filled my moments away from it with immense joy; her very existence is a precious gift.

Lorraine Byrne Bodley,
Dublin,
February 2013

BIOGRAPHIES

Seóirse Bodley (DMus) born Dublin in 1933. Studies in Ireland and Germany (Staatliche Hochschule für Musik, Stuttgart) were followed by an appointment in the Music Department of University College Dublin, of which he is now an Emeritus Professor. He is a founder-member of Aosdána, Ireland's academy of creative artists and was elected Saoi of Aosdána, one of the seven artists in different disciplines who can be elected to this honour, and the first composer to receive it.

His works include five symphonies for full orchestra, two chamber symphonies and numerous orchestral, choral, vocal and chamber pieces. The many major commissions he has received include his Third Symphony, commissioned for the opening of the National Concert Hall in Dublin, and his Fourth Symphony, commissioned by the Arturo Toscanini Symphony Orchestra of Parma, Italy.

Awards include: Saoi of Aosdána (2008); President of the Association of Irish Composers (2007); Marten Toonder Award (1982); Macaulay Fellowship in Music Composition (1962); Travelling Studentship of the National University of Ireland (1962); Arts Council Prize for Composition (1956).

Since his early twenties, Seóirse Bodley's music has been broadcast and performed in Ireland, across European countries, North America, Australia, China and Japan. Influences on his compositions include a range of musical styles from the European avant-garde to Irish traditional music, and most recently a series of works arising from the philosophy of the Austrian-born philosopher, Karl Popper.

Throughout his life, he has performed as accompanist with such established performers as Bernadette Greevy and the renowned English tenor Ian Partridge (2002) and more recently with Sylvia O'Brien (soprano) as in the 75th birthday concert of his song-cycles arranged for him by the Hugh Lane Gallery, Dublin (April 2008), the premieres of the song-cycle, *The Hiding Places of Love* (Poems, Seamus Heaney) in Dublin (May 2011) and the *Gretchen* cycle (April 2012). He will also accompany Sylvia O'Brien, Owen Gilhooly and Imelda Drumm in the Dublin premiere of these Goethe settings to mark his 80th birthday and Ireland's holding of the EU presidency (April 2013).

Lorraine Byrne Bodley holds a PhD in Music and in German from University College Dublin, and has completed postdoctoral studies in German at Trinity College Dublin (2001-03) and further postdoctoral studies in Music at the National University of Ireland, Maynooth (2003-04). Dr Byrne Bodley is the first woman in Ireland to be conferred with a DMUS in Musicology, a higher doctorate on published work (NUI, 2012). Other awards include a DAAD Senior Academics Award (2010); an IRCHSS Post-Doctoral Scholarship (2001-03); a DAAD scholarship (2002) and the Goethe Prize of the English Goethe Society (2001).

Following her position as Head of Music in Mater Dei, Dublin City University (2004-05), she was appointed to a permanent Lectureship in Musicology at the National

University of Ireland (2005). In 2010 she was Guest Professor at the University of Leipzig and in 2012 she was appointed Senior Lecturer in Musicology at NUI Maynooth.

Dr Byrne Bodley is known internationally for her work on Schubert, on Goethe and Music and on German Song, on all of which she has published prolifically and lectured internationally (in German and in English) in Germany, Belgium, Russia, Canada, USA, UK and Ireland. She has published 10 books including: *Goethe and Zelter: Musical Dialogues* (Ashgate, 2009) which was named an Outstanding Academic Book of 2010 by *Choice* and has been widely acclaimed as an 'excellent translation' and 'a major contribution' to musicology and Goethean studies (*Music and Letters, The Schubertian, Choice, Modern Language Review*). Other publications include: *The Unknown Schubert* (Ashgate, 2008); *Proserpina: Goethe's Melodrama with Music by Carl Eberwein* (Carysfort Press, 2007) and *Schubert's Goethe Settings* (2003).

EDITORIAL NOTE

The three scores which follow present, with few changes, 'Wandrers Nachtlied' ('Über allen Gipfeln') composed in 2003; *Mignon und der Harfner* (2004) and *Gretchen* (2012). When preparing the scores for publication I amended a number of typographical errors in the original manuscript of *Gretchen*. In all three works I followed versions of Goethe's texts in the Münchner Ausgabe: 'Wandrers Nachtlied (Über allen Gipfeln)';[1] the texts for *Mignon und der Harfner* are from Goethe's novel, *Wilhelm Meisters Lehrjahre*, vol. 5[2] and the texts from *Gretchen* are as they appear in Goethe's *Faust 1*.[3] Any exceptions, all of which are listed below, fall under three headings. Firstly, the composer made elisions in 'Der König in Thule' from the *Gretchen* cycle where 'heil'gen' (bar 45) is preferred to 'heiligen' and in 'Wandrers Nachtlied' 'Vög'lein' (bar 12) to 'Vögelein'. Secondly, Bodley has taken licence with Goethe's text in the Domszene in the *Gretchen* cycle: ignoring the repetition of 'langen' (bar 255); and adding an additional line of the 'Dies irae' ('Quem patronum rogaturus' to the final choral passage bars 253-54). Finally, as this score is intended as a critical performance edition, we did not follow the older German orthography in four songs: in 'Heiß mich nicht reden' we preferred 'möchte' (l.4) to 'mögte' (*Mignon und der Harfner*, stanza 1, l.3, bar 74); in 'Kennst du das Land?', we exchanged 'mögt (stanza 1, l. 7 and stanza 2, l.13) for 'möcht' (*Mignon und der Harfner*, bars 217 and 239). Although these variants are pronounced the same, we realized that this might not be common knowledge among singers and decided to employ current orthography within the musical text rather than hope an editorial note to this effect would be read by all performers. For the same reason we mirrored these changes in the texts (and translations) for both song cycles in the appendices.

Lorraine Byrne Bodley, February 2013

---

[1] Johann Wolfgang von Goethe, *Sämtliche Werke* in 20 vols. ed. by Karl Richter in collaboration with Herbert Göpfert, Norbert Miller und Gerhard Sauder (Munich and Vienna: Carl Hanser Verlag, 1988); hereafter referred to as *Münchner Ausgabe* (*MA*). 'Wandrers Nachtlied' appears in: *MA* 2.1 'Erstes Weimarer Jahrzehnt' ed. by Hartmut Reinhardt (Munich and Vienna: Carl Henser Verlag, 1987), p.53.

[2] Ibid. *MA* 5, *Wilhelm Meisters Lehrjahre. Ein Roman* ed. by Hans-Jürgen Schings (Munich and Vienna: Carl Henser Verlag, 1988). The texts appear as follows: 'An die Türen', p. 335; 'Heiß mich nicht reden', p.359; 'Wer nie sein Brot', p.134; 'Kennst du das Land', pp.142-43; 'Wer sich der Einsamkeit ergibt', pp.135-36; 'So laßt mich scheinen bis ich werde', pp.517-18; 'Nur wer die Sehnsucht kennt', pp.238-39.

[3] Ibid. *MA* 6.1, 'Weimarer Klassik 1798-1806' ed. by Victor Lang (1986); *Faust 1*, pp.553-673. The texts appear as follows: 'Der König in Thule', pp.613-14; 'Gretchen am Spinnrade', p.663-64; 'Gretchens Bitte', pp.640-41; 'Domszene', pp.646-47; 'Meine Mutter, die Hur', p.668.

Crossing Thresholds: On Seóirse Bodley's Goethe Settings

The Remaking of Mignon

Since Goethe's Mignon first appeared in print, her character has captured the imagination of hundreds of artists: an influence which resonates two centuries later. Whereas Mignon's story has gained mythic status, it has a much more determinate beginning than any legend and, as Terence Cave's recent study has shown, it is a story which has flowered with extraordinary rapidity.[4] In Cave's words:

> [A]n enigma was posed that countless writers, readers, composers, performers and listeners have reverted to, either in an attempt to unravel it, or because it has the fascination of a problem that can be reformulated endlessly.[5]

Although this story was primarily a 19th century obsession, countless writers, artists and composers have returned to Mignon, exploiting her story and participating in its culture's discourse. It is surprising how many artists have responded to the Goethean character to frame their own versions of her tale. From Novalis to Clemens Brentano; from Franz Catel to Anton Muttenthaler; from Johann Gottfried Schadow to Wilhelm Friedrich von Schadow; from Spontini to Beethoven; from Eichendorff to Immermann; from Schubert to Schumann; from Ary Sheffer to Wilhelm Kaulbach; from Eduard Mörike to Adalbert Stifter; from Gérard de Nerval to Charles Baudelaire; from Honoré de Balzac to George Eliot; from Tchaikovsky to Alban Berg: all of these artists remade Mignon in their own image, maintaining her importance in the modern world. With this we are led to ask: Who is Goethe's Mignon? What inspired her story? What has drawn writers and composers to her? And why is her story still relevant two hundred years later?

From her entrance in *Wilhelm Meisters Lehrjahre*, Book Four, Chapter Two, Mignon is surrounded by an air of mystery. She emerges as a beautiful creature, who is dressed in exotic male clothes. As a result, Wilhelm is unsure of her sex and she evades his enquiries about her identity. She presents herself as Mignon, and when asked her age, she replies, 'Es hat sie niemal gezählt'.[6] She speaks in broken German, in a strange formal manner, bowing and placing her hands on her chest and temple. Wilhelm is immediately fascinated by her presence: 'Seine Augen und sein Herz wurden unwiderstehlich von dem geheimnisvollen Zustande dieses Wesens angezogen' (the mystery that surrounded her completely absorbed his mind and feelings).[7] He describes her as a child of twelve or thirteen, with striking features, though he observes how her forehead seems to veil some secret, and her mouth is too tight-lipped for her age. Some of the reasons for her apprehension emerge in this chapter when Wilhelm discovers the circus master striking Mignon, rescues her and takes her into his care. Gradually, the mystery surrounding the beautiful waif unfolds. In Book Eight, Chapter Three, the doctor informs us that when she

---

[4] Terence Cave, *Mignon's Afterlives. Crossing Cultures from Goethe to the Twenty-First Century* (Oxford: Oxford University Press, 2011).
[5] Ibid, p.234.
[6] *WML* II, 4, HA.,7, p.98.
[7] Ibid.

was very young she was abducted by a company of tightrope walkers (*Seiltänzer*). Frightened, and in return for protection, she made a promise to the Divine Mother never to reveal her past. In Book Eight, Chapter Nine this past is disclosed through the discovery that Mignon is the Harper's child; her mother, Sperata, was the Harper's sister. The incestuous relations between Mignon's parents, which took place in the absence of knowledge on both sides, was made possible by the false shame of their father, who was unwilling to acknowledge a sexual encounter late in life and had his daughter Sperata fostered. The Harper's insistence that nature gave no sign of any interdict on their love[8] challenges the fictional (and ethical) notion of the 'call of the blood': the mysterious awareness that is supposed to accompany potential acts of incest.[9] Through the Harper's plight Goethe suggests that the human horror of incest (which is not observed in other animals) is produced by the religious shame and guilt imparted to their child.[10] In Goethe's early notes on the character of Mignon (1793) the phrase 'Wahnsinn des Mißverhältnisses' alludes to her origins.[11] We are never told her baptismal name (although it could have easily emerged at the denouement): the name 'Mignon' is given to her as a street performer.[12]

Numerous tales of encounters with such real-life figures abound in 19th century cultural history. The first and founding case of an encounter with Mignon is Goethe's famous meeting with a wandering harpist and his loquacious 11-year-old daughter to whom Goethe gives a lift while on his way to Italy in 1786.[13] Before the discovery of the manuscript of *Wilhelm Meisters theatralische Sendung* it was thought that this meeting might have been the 'origin' of the Mignon strand in the novel,[14] but that turned out not

---

[8] For Augustine's defence of incest, see *WML* VIII, 9, pp.582-84, esp. p.584, where he uses the analogy of the bisexual lily, which bears both 'husband and wife' on the same stem. Nicholas Boyle picks up the reference to plant morphology and makes it central to his reading of the episode in *Goethe: The Poet and the Age*, vol.2, *Revolution and Renunciation* (1790-1803) (Oxford: Oxford University Press, 2000), pp.414-417.

[9] It also undermines in advance those twentieth century interpretations that ascribe Mignon's supposed mental and physical deficiencies including her hermaphroditic nature to the incest of her parents; see, for example Paul Kraus, 'Mignon, der Harfner, Sperata. Die Psychopathologie einer Sippe in *Wilhelm Meisters Lehrjahren*', *Deutsche Vierteljahresschrift*, 22(1944), pp.327-54. Mignon's androgynous nature and her incestuous origins are conflated by Caitriona MacLeod, *Embodying Ambiguity: Androgyny and Aesthetics from Winkelmann to Keller* (Detroit: Wayne State University Press, 1998), pp.105-7. McLeod's arguments are echoed by Cordula Grewe, 'Mignon also Allegorie des Poetischen: Goetherezeption und Kunsttheorie in der deutschen Malerei der Spätromantik' in *Goethe und das Zeitalter der Romantik*, ed. Walter Hinderer (Würzburg: Königshausen & Neumann, 2004), p.313.

[10] Gustave Cohen argues that Mignon's mysteriously 'defective' nature could only be explained by the assumption that she was born with indeterminate sexuality, that she was literally a hermaphrodite, 'Mignon', *Jahrbuch der Goethe-Gesellschaft* 7 (1920), pp.132-53.

[11] *WML* 616. The most likely sense of this enigmatic phrase is something like 'delusional mismatch [with the real world]' but the word 'Missverhältnis' could just possibly be taken to refer to a defective or inappropriate relationship, hence (in this case) incest. One should, however, remember that, in 1793, Goethe had only just returned to the novel he had left unfinished some years previously: it seems likely that the story of Augustin and Sperata, which is not narrated until Book VIII, was already firmly established as a point of reference for the denouement.

[12] For a detailed discussion of Goethe's reasons for choosing this name, see Fritze R. Lachmann, 'Goethes Mignon: Entstehung, Name, Gestaltung', *Germanisch-Romanische Monatschrift*, 15 (1927), pp.100-16.

[13] Goethe, *Italienische Reise*, in *Werke Kommentar und Register* ed. Erich Trunz (Munich: C.H.Beck, 1981), vol.xi, *Autobiographische Schriften*, III, pp.14-15. The girl is 'pleasant and natural' when she speaks and laughs; however, when she is silent, 'schien sie etwas zu bedeuten zu wollen und machte mit der Oberlippe eine fatale Miene' (she seemed to want to intimate something or other and made a portentous expression with her upper lip'), a description which is vaguely reminiscent of Mignon and her secret.

[14] For a detailed account of Mignon's appearance in *Wilhelm Meisters Theatralische Sendung*, see Nicholas Boyle, *Goethe: The Poet and the Age* vol.1. *The Poetry of Desire (1749-1790)* (Oxford: Oxford University Press, 1991), 267, 365-75, 399-406.

to be the case. Goethe had already invented Mignon before he met her, as is indeed indicated by a later reference in the diary to Mignon's homeland.[15] As Carolyn Steedman has persuasively shown, child street performers were a frequent and often disquieting sight in nineteenth-century European cities, and Goethe's encounter with a 'Mignon' and her older companion already crosses that threshold.[16]

When Goethe invented Mignon as an incidental character in his *Bildungsroman*, *Wilhelm Meisters Lehrjahre*, he drew on many literary traditions. As Jarno recognizes in the *Lehrjahre*, Mignon is *zwitterhaft*,[17] a hybrid form, situated on a number of thresholds, which can be located within her own narrative in cultural history (including both literary and musical history and the history of ideas). The traditional model for Mignon's alternative story is the romance, with its histories of child abduction, its mysteries of identity and ultimate recognition scenes. Such is the retrospective narrative delivered by the Marchese whose timely arrival at Mignon's funeral leads to the discovery of a birthmark on her arm and thus of her identity as his niece. The denouement of the story of Mignon and the Harpist in *Wilhelm Meisters Lehrjahre* is obedient to the conventions of the recognition narrative of romance: the arrival of a character able to perform the identification, the presence of a boldily mark, the story of old unhappiness and its dislocating consequences. Abduction, loss of identity, exile both physical and geographical, are the necessary preconditions of such anagnorisis. In Goethe's version, the recognition is posthumous but this falls within the class of deferred anagnorisis as defined in chapter 14 of Aristotle's *Poetics*, even if the effect of deferment is not as shattering as Sophocles' *Oedipus*. The poetics of anagnorisis is far from being a merely formal structure; it provides an archaeology and the beginnings of an anthropology. From *Iphigeneia among the Taurians* to Shakespeare's *Perdita* and Cervantes's *Gitanilla*, vulnerable young women displaced into a potentially threatening environment are rescued (usually but not always) by a timely anagnorisis. The extraordinary staying power of such stories draws on one of the fundamental aspects of human life: encounters with strange characters who have difficulties in making themselves understood, who have sorrows they are unwilling or unable to talk about, who might be hostile but who might have precious gifts or knowledge to offer. Such stories feature lost children, severance, abduction, sexual and economic exploitation. The famously enigmatic features of Goethe's Mignon are different from those of any archetype, more complex and unexpected, yet the origin of the enigma is enduring: it is the ancient story of a severance that makes possible cross-cultural encounters.

One of the archetypes on which Goethe draws is the hermaphrodite – a portrayal in which the ambiguity of gender is given such prominence in Goethe's presentation of Mignon that it has attracted a good deal of critical attention in recent times.[18] Mignon's

---

15 The encounter is recorded in the entry for 7 September; the reference to Mignon's homeland occurs in the entry for 22 September. For a possible analogy between Mignon and the 11-year-old Fritz von Stein (the son of Goethe's intimate friend Charlotte von Stein), who lived in Goethe's household from 1783-86, see Fritz R. Lachmann, 'Goethes Mignon: Entstehung, Name, Gestaltung', Germanisch-Romanische Monatschrfit 15 (1927), pp.100-16, here pp.101-5 and Carolyn Steedman, *Strange Dislocations: Childhood and the Idea of Human Interiority, 1780-1930* (London: Virago Books, 1995), p.28.

16 A further example is found in Heinrich Heine, *Sämtliche Werke*, vol. vii,1, *Reisebilder III-IV*, ed. Alfred Opitz (Hamburg: Hoffmann und Campe, 1986), pp.47-52. Julia König provides an extensive analysis of the Mignon motif in Bettina von Armim's *Briefwechsel mit einem Kind* (1835) in *Das Leben im Kunstwerk. Studien zu Goethes Mignon und ihrer Rezeption* (Frankfurt: Peter Lang, 1991), pp.213-53.

17 WML III, 11, p.193: 'Ich hab' es oft mit Ekel und Verdruß gesehen, wie Sie...Ihr Herz an einen herumziehenden Bänkelsänger und an ein albernes, zwitterhaftes Geschöpf hängen mussten' (I have often noticed with disgust and annoyance that you...felt obliged to attach your affections to a wandering street singer and a stupid, hybrid creature').

18 See in particular, Catriona MacLeod, *Embodying Ambiquity: Androgyny and Aesthetics from Winkelmann to Keller* (Detroit: Wayne State University Press, 1988) and Cordula Grewe,

name, which introduces her gender identity as male and female, is not only a feminine proper noun, but is the masculine and feminine form of the French word meaning 'darling'.[19] In *Wilhelm Meisters Lehrjahre* she is called *das Knabenmädchen* and in the *Theatralische Sendung* she is referred to as both he and she. Throughout the novel Goethe's Mignon hovers uncertainly in her sex; the uncertainty that surrounds her gender may be construed, at least in part, as a consequence of her physical immaturity: the pre-pubertal child was still widely considered in the eighteenth century to partake in both genders. As is traditional to the hermaphrodite, Mignon slips between male and female roles and her gender transpositions are meaningful in the development of her character. Mignon enters the narrative wearing boys' clothing,[20] the costume the tightrope walkers have given her and one which was customary for young female acrobats in the eighteenth century.[21] She subsequently exchanges that costume for a uniform that designates her as Wilhelm's personal servant or page-boy. This role as Wilhelm's devoted servant, wearing her master's colours[22] is also laden with significance, for the French noun *mignon* was also widely known in the eighteenth century to mean 'sexually favoured male courtier' (initially the favourites of the late sixteenth-century French king Henri III).[23] Interestingly, McLeod points out that Goethe saw cross-dressing as an intrinsically theatrical phenomenon[24] and assembles a body of evidence showing that the opposition or harmonization of 'male' and 'female' ideals of beauty is a recurrent motif of aesthetic theory of the late eighteenth and early nineteenth centuries.[25]

Goethe's portrayal of Mignon as hermaphrodite is influenced by the myths of Greek antiquity. In the eighteenth century sexual orientation was considered in relation to a person's gender rather than to what the individual desired. Yet one only had to look to classical and archaic society to realize the recent nature of this assumption. In Hellenic mythology nature and desire could differ, and while nature would have its way, it could not deny the desires of others, including the gods. The Greeks and early Romans seem to have shared in folk beliefs and practices that were more open in their epistemology of sexual nature and sexual culture. Their acceptance of sexual and gender variations emerged from fundamental sources, as Greek theogony most amply proves that all deities

'Mignon als Allegorie des Poetischen: Goetherezeption und Kunsttheorie in der deutschen Malerei der Spätromantik', in *Goethe und das Zeitalter der Romantik*, ed. Walter Hinderer (Würzburg: Königshausen & Neumann, 2002), pp.307-43 which draws extensively on MacLeod's study. Both of these critics are concerned with the relationship between literature and visual art; both presuppose a reading of *Wilhelm Meister* in which the 'androgynous' representation of Mignon is central. See also Michael Minden, *The German* Bildungsroman: *Incest and Inheritance* (Cambridge: Cambridge University Press, 1997), esp. pp.42-48 and Michael Wetzel, *Die Kindsbraut als Phantasma der Goethezeit* (Munich: Wilhelm Fink Verlag, 1999). For an earlier example of this critical perspective, see Marie Delcourt, 'Deux interpretations romanesques du mythe de l'androgyne: Mignon et Séraphita, *Revue des langues vivantes*, 38 (1972), pp.228-40, 340-47.

[19] In Italian, the adjective 'mignon' means 'miniature', while the French form translates as 'dainty'.
[20] Mignon's appearance in male clothing may also be drawn from the early Greek tradition, where boys dressed as girls and girls as boys in their major ceremonies of life.
[21] Steedman, *Strange Dislocations*, chap.6.
[22] See Lachmann, 'Goethes Mignon'; and Steedman, *Strange Dislocations*, 26. On homoerotic expression and behaviour in eighteenth-century Germany (but without reference to Mignon's name), see Daniel W. Wilson, 'But is it gay? Kissing, friendship and "pre-homosexual" discourses in eighteenth-century Germany', *Modern Language Review*, 103 (2008), pp.767-83.
[23] This exchange of genders is continually developed through the novel: in Book Four, Chapter Ten, Mignon is afraid of a surgeon, 'der sie bisher immer für einen Knaben gehalten hatte', *WML* IV, 10, *HA*., 7, pp.236-37; after her clothes were burnt in the fire Aurelie proposes that she should be dressed as a girl, which Mignon strongly resists, *WML* V, 15, *HA*, 7, p.336. Later in Book Seven, Chapter Four the physician relates that the Harper was afraid of Mignon before he found out she was a girl, *WML*, V, 15, *HA*.,7, p.437; the Marchese's comments are developed in *WML* VIII, 9, *HA*., 7, p.587.
[24] MacLeod, *Embodying Ambiguity*, pp.94-96.
[25] Ibid, Chapter 1.

are sexually ambiguous or have dual gender manifestations. This presentation of deities as androgynous forms is evident in the variety of life forms that Zeus could temporarily inhabit, at one time desiring a woman and later a boy. It is seen in the significance of the god Hermaphroditus, who was often equated historically with what we would today label the folk ideology of homosexuality. It is present in the acceptance of the legendary Tiresias, who changed from male to female to male again in one lifetime, and whose soothsaying powers hark back to such pansexuality.[26] Plato's idea of the three sexes in the *Symposium* no doubt had a bearing on the very different notions of culture and human nature in the Greek tradition, which allowed a greater latitude of exceptions to the later historical gendered self that was to emerge.[27] Goethe's adoption and development of this tradition reveals the extraordinary influence of the hermaphrodite in Western culture and art. His gynandrous portrayal of Mignon bears witness to the long emerging tension between systems of sexual classification and affirms how the phenomenological force of the idealized form grows the longer it exists within traditions of culture. By placing the hermaphrodite in a contemporary context, Goethe exposes the ineluctable tendency in society to dimorphize classical culture. Like the Greeks, Goethe recognizes fundamental differences between male and female, but his acceptance of hermaphroditism in human nature permits more fluidity in states of being and ways of human acting.

If these combined literary and mythical genres provide one major axis for Mignon's story, her songs provide another. In *Wilhelm Meisters Lehrjahre* music is recognized as a higher form of communication, a *symbolische Sprache*, capable of expressing the emotions of its creator.[28] It is the expression of Mignon's deepest self and, if her songs are merely seen as decorative inclusions in the novel, then their true nature, purpose, and value is misunderstood. Mignon's lieder, which are of a more varied character than those of the Harper,[29] are so bound up with the inner emotional life of the performers that it becomes impossible to think of song merely as an aesthetically pleasing and moving supplement to the serious nature of their lives.[30] When Mignon crosses the threshold to sing for Wilhelm in Book Three, her lied is true to the life of feelings in a way her language cannot be. Through Mignon's songs Goethe suggests how the laws of musical construction aid rather than impede emotional expression. In Book Eight, Chapter Nine it is revealed that as a child Mignon 'sang bald sehr artig und lernte die Zither gleichsam von sich selbst. Nur mit Worten konnte es sich nicht ausdrücken, und es schien das Hindernis mehr in seiner Denkungsart als in den Sprachwerkzeugen zu liegen' (sang very pleasingly, and soon learned by her own efforts to play the zither. But she could not express herself in words, and the obstacle seemed to be in her mind rather than in her speech organs).[31] Although Mignon remains aphasic, her music is highly expressive, and in her songs the real Mignon is found. Here Goethe recognizes how music is a genuine

[26] Traces of hermaphroditism can also be discerned in Adonis, Dionysos, Cybele, Castor and Pollux.

[27] This is particularly evident in Plato's depiction of the myth of sexuality in the *Symposium*, where, according to the character Aristophanes, there were originally wholes: all male, all female, male and female. Whereas each person seeking his other original half might be in search of the same or other sex, contemporary interpretations block out the homosexual wholes of Plato's parable.

[28] This theme of musical communication is developed in many of Goethe's literary works, see for example *Die Wahlverwandtschaften*, *Werther*, the *Novelle* and *Faust*. For the poet's affirmation of this idea, see Goethe's letters to Zelter on 19 October 1829, *Goethe Briefe*, 4, *HA.*, 7, Letter no. 1441, p.347 and on 28 June 1831, *Goethe Briefe*, 4, *HA.*, 7, Letter no.1497, pp.433-34.

[29] Even within the novel this element of Mignon's songs is noted as Serlo comments on the delightful variety of her singing, WML V, 1, HA.,7, p.283.

[30] For an interesting reading of Goethe's texts for the songs in *Wilhelm Meisters Lehrjahre* see Martina Kiess, *Poesie und Prosa. Die Lieder in 'Wilhelm Meisters Lehrjahren'* (Frankfurt am Main: Athenäum, 1987).

[31] *WML* VIII, 9, *HA.*,7, pp.586-87.

emotive language, which awakens certain definite emotions in the listener. Wilhelm is deeply moved by Mignon's renditions of 'Kennst du das Land' and 'Nur wer die Sehnsucht kennt'. Similarly, Natalie reports the grace and appeal of 'So laßt mich scheinen', where the strange unearthly charm of her character is conveyed through her song. Like the Harpist, Mignon is an embodiment of an aesthetic domain; she offers a secularized, naturalistic way of understanding the relation of song to human experience. How closely bound up Mignon is with song is evident in the *Wanderjahre* where Wilhelm spends three days on Lake Maggiore, with three companions, one of whom is an accomplished amateur singer. On the third evening, he sings Mignon's 'Kennst du das Land?'; the effect it has on Wilhelm and others gathered shows that Goethe recognized the power of Mignon's signature tune as a marker for everything she represents: severance, the impossible longing for restitution, the intensity and fragility, and the power of song to embody all of these. The song erupts, expected yet unheralded, the effect anticipating the Proustian convergence of conscious memory with a *mémoire involuntaire* triggered by some sensual or aesthetic experience. What Goethe stages in this extraordinary episode is the real Mignon, the one who inhabits song.

In conclusion, Goethe's Mignon is a strange, complex, conflicted creature: a child born into a noble family who is now a homeless wanderer; a street performer, dancer and acrobat, a singer who is aphasic; a vulnerable girl on the brink of sexual maturity; a fragile and overwrought young woman subject to seizures; an angelic being doomed to an early death who is given a secular funeral. She and her behaviour are repeatedly referred to as 'geheimnisvoll' (mysterious, secretive) or 'seltsam' (strange) and she keeps to herself a secret that is only fully uncovered after her death. Literally and dramatically when Mignon crosses Wilhelm's threshold at the opening of Book Three that moment brings together in a single scenario her position between aphasia and expression, between different cultural worlds (Italian and German, untaught and polished), between childlike dependence on a father figure and the beginnings of erotic desire, between a child who communicates with difficulty and a young woman who has taken a mysterious oath of silence; between a worldly *Sehnsucht* and an aspiration to an unreachable higher sphere. The impact Mignon has had on readers and later composers (not to mention singers and their audience) depends on the co-existence of all these strands.

A Myth Appropriated: Greek Orpheus to Goethe's Harper

Goethe's Harper, inspired by the Orpheus of classical mythology, is also a complex, multifaceted figure. For the ancients Orpheus is an archetypal poet, yet his name is linked with mystery religion and illumination. The portrayal of the Harper as hierophant is suggested in *Wilhelm Meisters Lehrjahre*, where he is presented as a poet-prophet. Through his suffering the Harper travels to the world beyond and emerges as a master of life's mysteries. His songs show insight into the suffering of men and in performance this knowledge is communicated to others.[32] While the Harper's portrayal as priest inevitably overlaps with the founder of Orphism, it is the Orpheus of the musical tradition that Goethe primarily presents. In classical mythology, Orpheus, 'best voice', is a musician and poet, who plays the lyre,[33] sings and, by skilful modulation of his voice, obtains Eurydice. In *Wilhelm Meisters Lehrjahre* the Harper is known for the beauty and power of his voice, and his relationship with Sperata commences in song.[34] In ancient Greece,

---

[32] See for example Wilhelm's response to the Harper's song, *WML* II, 11 *HA.*,7, p.128; *WML* II, 14, *HA.*,7, p.137 and *WML* IV, 12, *HA.*, 7, p.240.

[33] In some versions of the myth, Orpheus plays the cithara. In associating Mignon with this instrument, Goethe insinuates her connections with the Harper.

[34] In the Marchese's account of the Harper's tale he acknowledges: 'daß Gesang und Musik unsern Bruder schon bei ihr (Sperata) eingeführt hatten', *WML* VIII, 9, *HA.*, 7, p.582, an opinion endorsed by Goethe's Harper relates how 'beide Gemüter gleich beiden Kehlen zusammen stimmten', *WML* VIII, 9, *HA.*, 7, p.583.

Orpheus is portrayed as a magician, the practitioner of a mysteriously compelling incantatory force, whose music bewitches gods, men, animals and even inanimate objects such as stones and mountains. In *Wilhelm Meisters Lehrjahre* the Harper's powers are mythical, not magical. He is presented as an artist, an enchanting musician, who charms people with the beauty of his song. In the Hellenic myth, wisdom is usually associated with the Harper because of his gift of oration – a naturalness of speech which is remarked upon by Wilhelm. Whereas music gives the Harper the means to unite all men, he is also the marginal figure of the classical myth. Like the Thracian poet, he emerges as an asocial figure, isolated by the fact that he feels and suffers with the totality of his being. In Book Five, Chapter Sixteen the Abbé tries to reintegrate the Harper into the community, yet like the classical persona, he remains a peripheral figure, with no return to a well-defined social identity. In portrayals of the legend there is in Orpheus an intentional lack of stress on individualizing physical details, a representation which is continued in Goethe's novel, where he is identified metonymically – der Harfner – and all the other epithets succeed in making an abstraction of him. Although young like Orpheus, he is presented as an old man,[35] his unkempt appearance indicative of his liminal status. Whereas the classical harpist is located in an open landscape, in Goethe's metamorphosis of this myth he is placed indoors.[36] Through this association, the images of confinement are reinforced and this prison is metaphorical of his mental state. In Book Two, Chapter Thirteen, when Wilhelm goes in search of the Harper, he is directed to 'ein schlechtes Wirtshaus in einem entfernten Winkel des Städtchens' (a shabby inn in a remote part of the town)[37] and the Harper's music emerges from behind closed doors. In classical mythology Orpheus is portrayed as a wanderer, who, on the expedition of the Argonauts, uses his art to overcome the melody of the sirens and return his companions to the straight path. In *Wilhelm Meisters Lehrjahre* the Harper enters as an itinerant musician, 'ein hülfreicher Schutzgeist' (a protective spirit),[38] whose music is connected with the divine, yet he also suffers at the hands of the gods. Like Orpheus, he suffers the loss of the beloved and endures inconsolable grief. As Hermes cannot bring a happy omen to Orpheus and Eurydice's wedding, there is no good omen for the Harper's marriage to Sperata.[39]

Before Virgil, Orpheus embodied the power of music over animate and inanimate nature, its civilizing power, and, as an extension of its healing spell, its ability to cross the divide between life and death. In Virgil's *Georgics*, however, the story of Orpheus becomes a tragedy of human passion, and in *Wilhelm Meisters Lehrjahre* this aspect is revealed. As in the *Georgics*,[40] Goethe makes the Harper a tragic lover, who is the victim of madness and of love together. Virgil's Orpheus loses Eurydice, when his passion yields to *dementia* and *furor* (488; 495), he disobeys the inexorable laws of nature and suffers accordingly. Like Virgil, Goethe stresses the disastrous passion and desperate madness of

---

[35] When the Harper is introduced into the novel his description bears the signs of age, *WML* II, 11, *HA.*,7, p.128, and throughout the novel he is continually referred to as 'der Alte': *WML* II, 11, *HA.*,7, p.128; *WML* III, 6, p.169; *WML* IV, 1, pp.208-209; *WML* V, 13, p.332; *WML* V, 14, p.335; *WML* V, 15 p.335; *WML* V, 16, p.347 and *WML* VII, 8, p.489. When the Harper is reintegrated into society, there are no signs of age in his features, *WML* VIII, 10, *HA.*,7, p.595.

[36] See *WML* II, 11, *HA.*,7, p.127f. and *WML* II, 13, *HA.*,7, p.136f.; *WML* IV, 1, *HA.*, 7, pp.208-9; *WML* IV, 12, *HA.*, 7, pp.240-41; *WML* V, 13, *HA.*, 7, pp.330-31 and *WML* V, 16, *HA.*,7, pp.346-47. Even the chapters where the Harper is placed outdoors are dominated by images of captivity: in *WML* V, 14, the Harper is trapped by insanity (*HA.*,7, pp.334-35) and though he is placed in the middle of a lake, which in itself is an image of isolation, the boatsman ferries him back to the monastery , *WML* VIII, 9, *HA.*,7, p.585.

[37] *WML* II, 13, *HA.*, 7, p.136.

[38] *WML* II, 11, *HA.*, 7, p129.

[39] *WML* VIII, 9, *HA.*, 7, pp.582-83.

[40] Virgil, *Georgics* 4, ll.494-8.

a love which violates social law, and is punished by eternal separation.[41] In the *Georgics* Virgil lays little emphasis on the poetic side of Orpheus; it is subordinated entirely to the theme of unwise passion and uncreative grief. Goethe differs from Virgil in the unity of his adaptation and the Harper emerges as poet, lover, and priest. In *Georgics* 4, Virgil tells the story of Orpheus's tragic loss of Eurydice and the inconsolable mourning that marked his pathetic life thereafter. In *Wilhelm Meisters Lehrjahre* the Harper's sorrow is protracted, yet it is recognized as an essentially futile and ultimately suicidal grief for a loss which cannot be altered. Like Virgil's Orpheus, the Harper never analyses or understands his grief and so, continually indulged, his misery becomes an emblem of inertia and death. In Virgil's *Georgics* Orpheus is guilty for looking back at Eurydice and his 'madness' causes him to lose Eurydice. In *Wilhelm Meisters Lehrjahre* the Harper has turned away from the love of a woman and Mignon's presence underlines the reason for his guilt. As Eurydice is passive in Virgil, Sperata is subject in *Wilhelm Meisters Lehrjahre*. With that our attention shifts to the Harper and his pathetic situation, where his feelings of love and loss are compounded by an inevitable sense of guilt. Whereas Virgil observes Orpheus's connection with Hades, the idea of an Underworld is at variance with Goethe's thinking. In *Wilhelm Meisters Lehrjahre* the Harper never descends; his hell is on earth and his dark torment is depicted through imagery of the abyss. In Book Seven, Chapter Four the physician describes him in relation to this void:

> bloß in sich gekehrt, betrachtete er sein hohles, leeres Ich, das ihm als ein unermeßlicher Abgrund erschien[42]

> completely shut up in himself, he looked at his hollow and empty self, which seemed to him like a bottomless pit

which the Harper himself confirms:

> Ich sehe nichts vor mir, nichts hinter mir als eine unendliche Nacht, in der ich mich in der schrecklichsten Einsamkeit befinde; [...] Doch da ist keine Höhe, keine Tiefe, kein Vor und Zurück, kein Wort drückt diesen immer gleichen Zustand aus. Manchmal ruf ich in der Not dieser Gleichgültigkeit: Ewig! ewig! mit Heftigkeit aus, und dieses seltsame, unbegreifliche Wort ist hell und klar gegen die Finsternis meines Zustandes.[43]

> I see nothing before me, and nothing behind me [...] nothing but the endless night of loneliness in which I find myself [...] There is no height or depth, no forwards or backwards, nothing to describe this continual sameness. Sometimes I cry out 'forever, forever' in the face of this terrifying indifference, and that strange incomprehensible word is a beacon of light in the darkness of my condition.

The polarity between the lone singer and the terrible powers of the underworld, as suggested by Virgil, is portrayed in 'Wer nie sein Brot' mit Tränen', and in Book Seven Chapter Four, the Harper relates: 'Kein Strahl einer Gottheit erscheint mir in dieser Nacht' (No gleam of any godhead comes to me in this dark night).[44] Unlike Virgil's Orpheus, the Harper faces the gods not as an heroic bard, but as a single mortal armed only with his art and his love. By developing the human side of the Harper more fully than Virgil, Goethe makes the contrast more pointed. As in the Augustan age, Goethe uses myth as a literary tool to explore the human soul, and the blend of sympathy and blame is present in Goethe as in Virgil. While he is sensitive to the Harper and associates his distress with human inadequacy, the irreconcilables, the unbridgeable gulf between soul and instinct, nevertheless remain.

Although described in different ways in legends and in verse, the portrayal of Orpheus as the pre-eminent musician is ubiquitous. In Goethe's metamorphosis of this myth, the

---

[41]Whereas Ovid's *Metamorphosis* rules out the powerful theme of *furor* and all the guilt which accompanies Orpheus's lament, it is intriguing to note that the songs of Ovid's grieving Orpheus deal mainly with incestuous love, Ovid, 10, ll. 148-739.

[42] *WML* VII, 4, *HA.*, 7, p.436

[43] Ibid.

[44] Ibid.

Harper emerges as the very personification of the power of music. His is the voice of Music and his role is that of Music Incarnate. In *Wilhelm Meisters Lehrjahre* the symbol of the Harpist follows that of his instrument. The lyre possesses a purely literal meaning of the attribution of musical gifts to the Harper, which holds further significance when it is applied to the psychological and spiritual plane. The sound of the harp symbolizes the quest for happiness, of which the Harper knows only the fragile assurances of this world. In Greek mythology it is the harp that the gods or their messengers play, which irresistibly lulls its hearers to sleep and occasionally ushers them into the Beyond. Although the Harper does not lead his listeners into another world, his song soothes them to sleep: [45] as Mignon and the Harper sing 'Nur wer die Sehnsucht kennt', Wilhelm 'verfiel in eine träumende Sehnsucht'.[46] For Goethe there are the two types of music: divine music as the music of the spheres and the *imagines* of the divine music in the human soul. In the Harper's songs of lamentation, Goethe plays on the latter: in the introductions to his songs he gives the impression that he waits till he hears the music and then performs. Through this portrayal Goethe suggests how music is not merely connected with sound, but with a state of mind, of being.

Like Mignon, Goethe's Harper is an amalgam of influences, and his name, Augustine, is laden with significance, especially when one realizes that Goethe was born in 1749 on the Feast of St Augustine, the patron saint's *Todestag*, 28 August 430, suggesting the Harper, like Werther, gives voice to something in the poet's experience. In different ways the Harper – like Wilhelm and Faust – are the literary realization of Augustine's anthropology, announced in the opening lines of his *Confessions:* 'You have made us, O Lord, for yourself and our heart is restless until it rests in you'. All three figures exemplify Augustine's restless heart, whose nourishment is not earthly and who continue to strive and err, until they reach a state of Divine clarity. In the *Confessions* Augustine habitually shows himself little mercy. Most significantly, the Harper's suffering, which is the consequence of a separation conflict from Sperata – wanting to stay with her through love and feeling it necessary to leave – can be read as a literary reflection of St Augustine's fifteen-year monogamous relationship to his concubine, the mother of Adeodatus, whom he describes in the *Confessions* as 'the only one for me'. Augustine's subsequent manumission of her in favour of a socially upward marriage is described in the *Confessions* 6.15, where he relates:

> The woman with whom I habitually slept was torn from my side because she was a hindrance to my marriage. My heart, which was deeply attached to her, was cut and wounded, and left a trail of blood. She returned to Africa, vowing never to go with another man. She left me with the natural son I had by her. But I was unhappy [...] my wound inflicted by the parting was not healed. After inflammation and sharp pain, it festered. The pain made me as it were frigid but desperate.[47]

Despite this severance, Augustine's 'wandering desire' remained very much directed to her and he mourned her loss over a decade later. In the writings of 386 the wound still throbs and the grief of his lacerated, undivided heart is unmistakeable. Women, sexual relations and guilt are intimately connected within the matrix of meanings that constitute Goethe's Harper and Augustine's writing on women, whose anthropology is still one of the platforms of orthodoxy within Catholicism. In defining *Sapientia* as masculine, Augustine defied a long history of religious tradition that had perceived Wisdom as feminine,[48] a tradition Goethe continually endorses. Augustine's position is at once present and questioned in the Harper's songs, where 'Wer sich der Einsamkeit ergibt' is connected with the Greek *paramythia* and the Latin *consolatio*. In the Christian

---

[45] *WML* II, 11, *HA.*, 7, pp.128-30.
[46] *WML* IV, 12, *HA.*, 7, p.240.
[47] *Confessions*, 6, 15, *Patrologia Latina* ed. J.P.Migne (Paris, 1878-1890), 32, 732.
[48] E. Neumann, *Man and Woman in Christian Perspective* (London: Hodder and Stoughton, 1990), p.58.

tradition, the poet is equipped with arguments to console for death, exile and other misfortunes of this world. In comparison with this genre, the Harper has lost faith and hope, and has no one to turn to for consolation. Renouncing his name (Augustin) and all it signifies, his anguish is deepened with the realization of consolations denied. Goethe's composition of 'Wer sich der Einsamkeit ergibt' is also suggestive of the tradition of meditative exercises which were begun by St. Augustine. Unlike the elegiac lament which begins with the first person formula, the meditative tradition begins with a question which is contemplated. In 'Wer sich der Einsamkeit ergibt' the proposal of such a question – an almost rhetorical question – parallels the questions that are typically found in the meditative sections of the *Confessions* and *De Trinitate*. The Harper's songs can be read as stations of grief: anger as the second stage of grief is subtly voiced in 'Wer nie sein Brot' while the bargaining stage of grief, announced in 'Wer sich der Einsamkeit ergibt', is an echo of Augustine's *Confessions* where Augustine trades exclusive love of God for freedom from grief: 'When at last I cling to you with all my being, for me there will be no more sorrow, no more toil. Then at last I shall be alive with true life, for my life will be wholly filled with you.'[49] Whether or not Augustine ever reached that fourth stage of true acceptance, the depression and pain that resonate in the rhetoric of these lines are echoed in the Harper's trilogy, where he is resigned to a *fait accompli*.

Seóirse Bodley, *Mignon und der Harfner* (2004)

The enigma which lies at the heart of the Harper and Mignon's story is the reason why composers have repeatedly returned to these figures: Zelter composed four different settings of Mignon's 'Kennst du das Land?'; the four settings by Beethoven and six by Schubert of 'Nur wer die Sehnsucht kennt' are further examples of composers' attempts to unravel her mystery. Whereas this music genealogy is not one I wish to follow here, I do wish to identify the uniqueness of Bodley's cycle, for only three other possible *Wilhelm Meister Lehrjahre* cycles can be identified. While Schumann's *Wilhelm Meister* songs are seldom described as a cycle, in the Hyperion recording of the complete Schumann songs, the pianist and scholar, Graham Johnson, convincingly proposes the set as a cycle, analysing the way it is structured in musical and narrative terms. In this cycle the order of settings deviates from the order of songs as they appear in Goethe's novel, yet Schumann does observe the chronology of Mignon and the Harper's songs within this cycle:

Table 1: Schumann's *Wilhelm Meisters Lehrjahre* Cycle:

	Song Title	Original Place in the Novel	Order of Mignon and Harper songs
M:	'Kennst du das Land?'	4	M1
H:	'Was hör ich draußen?'	1	H1
M:	'Nur wer die Sehnsucht kennt'	5	M2
H:	'Wer nie sein Brot'	2	H2
M:	'Heiß mich nicht reden'	8	M3
H:	'Wer sich der Einsamkeit'	3	H3
P:	'Singet nicht'	6	
H:	'An die Türen'	7	H4
M:	'So laßt mich scheinen'	9	M4
	Mignon's Requiem		

---

[49] *Confessions*, 10, 28; *Patrologia Latina* 32, 795.

The second possible *Lehrjahre* cycle is that of Hugo Wolf, who adopts a different order again. Here the Harper's three melancholy songs open the cycle with 'An die Türen', which is placed second, thus breaking the original order of the Harper's songs. Wolf's inclusion of the satirical *Spottlied* from the *Lehrjahre* III, 9, provides a violent contrast before three of Mignon's songs ('Heiss mich nicht reden', 'Nur wer die Sehnsucht kennt', 'So laßt mich scheinen'). Philine's song breaks the mood again before Mignon's signature tune 'Kennst du das Land?' and the Harper's ballad. The third cycle and the most scrupulous in respecting the original content is Anton Rubenstein's *Die Gedichte und das Requiem für Mignon aus Goethes Wilhelm Meisters Lehrjahre in Musik gesetzt* (op.91). Here Rubenstein not only sets the standard songs of Mignon, the Harpist, and Philine, but also the *Spottlied*, the Harpist's 'Ihm färbt der Morgensonne Licht' from IV, 1, the fragment 'Ich hatt' ihn einzig mir erkoren'; from the 'Bekenntnisse einer schönen Seele' (VI, 1), Mignon's requiem, and Friedrich's song 'O, ihr werdet Wunder sehn!' from Book Eight, Chapter Ten. The songs and requiem follow also the order in which they appear in the novel and 'Nur wer die Sehnsucht kennt' is correctly set as a duet. The only lapse in fidelity is the ascription of 'Ich hatt' ihn einzig mir erkoren' to Aurelie, whereas in fact it records the *innamoramento* of the anonymous 'schöne Seele'.

The original idea for a cycle based on the songs of Mignon and the Harper – as opposed to the *Lehrjahre* settings in general – originated in Bodley's attendance at a series of lectures I gave on 'Goethe and Music' at the Goethe Institute Dublin. The second and third lecture-recitals in this series which took place 4 and 11 May 2000 examined Schubert's Settings from Goethe's *Wilhelm Meisters Lehrjahre*: 'The Mignon Lieder' and 'The Harfner Songs', performed by Maire Mularkie (soprano), Roland Davitt (baritone) and accompanied by Claire Flynn (piano). Following this lecture series Bodley read *Wilhlem Meisters Lehrjahre* in its original German text. Three years later the cycle was commissioned for the conference, *Goethe: Musical Poet, Musical Catalyst* in NUI Maynooth, the premiere given by Kathleen Tynan (soprano), Sam McElroy (baritone) and Dearbhla Collins (piano) on 27 March 2004.

Bodley's cycle takes Goethe's novel as its point of departure. Just as Mignon and the Harper converge in Book Two, Bodley alternates the songs of each of these characters loosely reflecting the intermittent strands of the plot they occupy:

Table 2: Seóirse Bodley's *Mignon und der Harfner*

	Song Title	Original Place in the Novel
H:	'An die Türen'	7
M:	'Heiß mich nicht reden'	8
H:	'Wer nie sein Brot'	2
M:	'Kennst du das Land?'	4
H:	'Wer sich der Einsamkeit'	3
M:	'So laßt mich scheinen'	9
H & M:	'Nur wer die Sehnsucht kennt'	5

When Goethe came to order his poems in the collected edition of his works for Cotta in 1815, he himself presented them in an order quite different from the sequence in which they occur in the novel: 'Heiß mich nicht reden' comes first, followed by 'Nur wer die Sehnsucht kennt', 'So laßt mich scheinen', the Harper's three shorter songs and Philine's song. The epigraph which this section bears in Goethe's collection – 'Auch vernehmet im

Gedränge / Jeder Genien Gesänge' (Hear too, amid the crush, the songs of those inspired souls') – [50] could easily be applied to Bodley's cycle.

Whereas some of the most distinguished musical minds of the nineteenth-century had invented a musical voice for Mignon which echoes over Europe and beyond, Bodley was undaunted by her Romantic musical lineage and attracted to the modernity of her musical voice. Although a figure of the 19th century, wherever she travels, whether fictionally across the alps into unknown territory or across genres in musical history, Mignon remains on the borders, unresolved. This unsettling threshold which Mignon and the Harper occupy and their portrayal as figures of painful productive tension is immediately voiced in Bodley's setting of their songs where the dark internal brooding of the Harper contrasts wonderfully with Mignon's irregularity of character. The musical techniques Bodley employs relate to some degree to the character of the singers, especially that of Mignon. Their music shares its origins in a twelve-note row with four additional moveable notes – thus forming a flexible sixteen-note row:

Musical Example 1: Bodley, *Mignon und der Harfner*, Basic Series

Rhythmically there is a high degree of irregularity – most noticeable in Mignon's 'Heiss mich nicht reden'. In Bodley's cycle Mignon crosses a new threshold and finds another world to inhabit: in his cycle Mignon is a child of our time, the message she relays, intrinsically complex and plural.

'An die Türen will ich schleichen'

As with the Harper's other lyrics, 'An die Türen' was first published in *Wilhelm Meisters Lehrjahre* and was later included in Goethe's *Werke* of 1815. The poem is not included in the *Theatralische Sendung*.

Goethe's poem appears at the end of Book Five, Chapter Fourteen. In this chapter Wilhelm is deeply troubled about the fate of the Harper, who has disappeared since the fire. As he ponders upon his fate, he hears someone approaching nearby:

> An dem traurigen Gesange, der sogleich angestimmt ward, erkannte er den Harfenspieler. Das Lied, das er sehr wohl verstehen konnte, enthielt den Trost eines Unglücklichen, der sich dem Wahnsinne ganz nahe fühlt. Leider hat Wilhelm davon nur die letzte Strophe behalten: 'An die Türen will ich schleichen'.[51]

> From the mournful strains which had just sounded, he recognised the Harper. The very song which he could clearly understand was about the consolations of someone who feels he is very near to madness. Unfortunately Wilhelm could only remember the last verse: 'An die Türen will ich schleichen'.

At the end of this song the Harper reaches a locked gate. Seeking to escape, he tries to climb over the fence. When Wilhelm restrains him, the Harper requests that Wilhelm should open the gate for him 'weil er fliehen wolle und müsse' (because he wanted to indeed had to escape).[52] Wilhelm tries to reason with him, yet to no avail. Eventually, he drags him forcibly with him to the pavilion, 'schloß sich daselbst mit ihm ein und führte ein wunderbares Gespräch mit ihm' (shut himself up with [the Harper] and had an

---

[50] The phrase 'im Gedränge' has given rise to considerable discussion: is the 'crush' that of all the other poems in the collection, or is Goethe referring to the pressures of the everyday, the crowded city? Since 'auch' can be taken with 'im Gedränge' which changes the sense to 'Hear, amid the crush', the second of these readings seems more plausible.

[51] *WML* V, 14, *HA.*, 7, pp.334-35

[52] *WML* V, 15, *HA.*, 7, p.335.

extraordinary conversation with him), the content of which remains undisclosed. While the context of the Harper's song places him in the role of the wanderer, the images of captivity and restraint are illustrative of the theme of impending madness, alluded to in this song.[53]

'An die Türen' is composed as a single strophe, divided into two quatrains. The lines are written in trochaic tetrameter, with the final unstressed beat dropped in lines two, four, six and eight. The lines are syllabic with lines one, three, five and seven containing eight syllables, while the alternate lines each contain seven syllables. The rhyming scheme is *ababcdcd*.

Goethe's depiction of the Harper's irrationality reflects the prototypes of madness in Greek mythology. The classical representation of madness is dominated by three images: darkness, wandering, and guilt. In Latin *error* means wandering, veering off course, and in Greek 'wandering' carries negative overtones, meaning chaotic displacement. The earliest mad wanderer is Bellerophon, who, detested by the gods, wandered over the Aleian plain. In 'An die Türen' this association is continued, where the gods are depicted as the authors of human movement. Like Bellerophon, the gods inflict a centrifugal wandering on the Harper because they are punishing him. His suffering is associated with daemonic persecution and the poem portrays the Harper's desperate quest for inner peace. Like Orpheus, his self-detachment from others is depicted in the opening lines of the lyric, where his depiction as wanderer reveals how he seeks to escape from himself and from this burdening sense of guilt. In 'An die Türen' the dark portrayal of the Harper as wanderer signifies his search for release from the madness of obsessive guilt. Like Orestes, the Harper's madness arises through conflicting feelings regarding responsibility and guilt and is portrayed as punishment for human transgression of divine law. In 'An die Türen' Goethe suggests how the gods themselves can cause transgression, yet it does not diminish the Harper's responsibility. Like Sophocles' *Ajax* his madness is treated as essentially individual, a personal alienation from accepted social and political conduct. The poem portrays the Harper's struggle to apprehend and define the self in its dynamic relation to external reality, and the inner world he has created is an inversion of the reality he has known. As with Sophocles' *Ajax*, the Harper's madness and withdrawal from other human beings is portrayed as sickness, a state of mind that ultimately leads to his death.

In its literary context Goethe alters the traditional images of animality to captivity, and the Harper's song depicts the condition of madness as essential freedom constrained where madness is portrayed as a psychic goal; isolation and estrangement are the conditions he finds inescapable. As he concludes the final verse of 'An die Türen', the Harper reaches the garden gate:

> er wollte, da er sie verschlossen fand, an den Spalieren übersteigen; allein Wilhelm hielt ihn zürück [...] Der Alte bat ihn, aufzuschließen, weil er fliehen wolle und müsse.[54]
> Since he found it locked, he tried to climb over the fence, but Wilhelm held him back [...] The old man asked him to open the gate because he wanted to, indeed had to escape.

The Harper's gradual transformation into a primitive, bestial state is an unconscious one – a retreat to archaic cognitive and behavioural patterns as an escape from an unendurable situation, in an effort to 'preserve' some form in which survival is possible. In conceiving madness as a symbol of individual regression for survival, it is portrayed as a psychic defence; a flight from emotional duress.[55] While Goethe's portrayal of madness

---

[53] The theme of madness is referred to immediately before this song and in the opening sentence of Chapter Fifteen: 'Aus der großen Verlegenheit, worin sich Wilhelm befand, was er mit dem unglücklichen Alten beginnen sollte, der so deutliche Spuren des Wahnsinns zeigte', *WML* V, 14, *HA.*, 7, p.335.

[54] *WML* V, 14, *HA.*, 7, p.335.

[55] Other characteristics shared with Greek mythology include the linking of madness with the special sight (insight, foresight) of melancholia. In classical mythology the variety of com-

is drawn from classical mythology, his depiction of the Harper's psychosis – like that of Büchner's *Lenz* – is extraordinarily 'modern'. The protagonist of the poem is not a manic but a rational being who has repeatedly endured, remembers all too well, and lives in continual dread of psychic dissolution. In 'An die Türen' Goethe examines the unconscious conflicts that produce the Harper's madness, which extreme human and natural stimuli have released. His depiction of madness not only exposes the manifestation of human self-deception and pride but traces their roots in psychic conflict for which there is no implicit moral resolution. The poem portrays madness as the perpetual amorphous threat within; the extreme of the unknown. It is a fascinating exposure of the structures of irrational fears and bizarre desires ordinarily hidden from the self and the world.

In 'An die Türen' the Harper's madness is portrayed as an antithetical daemonic force within the self. One etymology of *daimōn* is *daiō*, 'I divide' which suggests that the daemonic is essentially divergent. The multiplicity and divisions of the divinity are an essential aspect of tragic in the Harper and he emerges a figure of opposites, paradox and contradiction. Within the context of the novel, Goethe's Harper embodies the antithesis Apollonian-Dionysian: an aesthetic theory of the Dionysian in contrast to the Apollonian as an unrestrained, intoxicated power of creation in the artist and the poetic genius. In his opening song in the novel, 'Der Sänger', he is connected with the extreme union of all possibilities, limitless gratification, power, wisdom and love. Yet Apollo and all the symbols of light and art to which he is consciously committed do not protect him against his knowledge of the deep threatening creation, natural and aesthetic, which are inherent in it. Here in 'An die Türen' Goethe exposes this dark side of the mind and portrays the Harper's identification with the dark and the chaotic. His song is not only a confrontation with himself, but a recognition of the elemental forces of violence and destruction in life. The Harper's experience of this realm is here portrayed through metaphors of driving forces as he is driven by ambiguous impulses toward destruction. The poem portrays the dramatic conflict between the forces of life and mind: an eternal tension, which the Harper cannot resolve. Whereas in his opening song, 'Der Sänger', the harper emerges as a symbol of the potential freedom of human beings in harmony with nature, in order to achieve this level of freedom the Harper must attain self-knowledge. Here in 'An die Türen', the Harper's vision is limited by the enormity of his personal grief and so he cannot make the wider application of his experience. Paradoxically, though the Harper emerges from classical mythology, he is a poet of feeling whose pretences to classical form are ineffective.

Seóirse Bodley, 'An die Türen will ich schleichen'

Bodley's decision to open the cycle with the portrayal of the Harper as Wanderer makes clear the role of symbols in human functioning. The primordial image or archetype – *der Wanderer, der Harfner, der Alte* – is a figure or process that emerges in human consciousness and is so universal that it repeats itself in the course of history and art. These mythical forms, which depict many human experiences, [56] arise out of an inherited potentiality – mnemic images – which are not innate ideas, but inborn possibilities of ideas. In the opening song of Bodley's cycle this archetype is stirred, his entrance heralded by the ominous bass octaves of the opening five bars. In the opening quatrain the Harper relates how he will steal up to people's doors. His furtive steps, the result of a

---

munication among the mad includes muteness (silence), violence, and suicide; in Goethe's Harper all three are combined.

[56] Goethe's depiction of the Harper, for example, may be based on Lenz, who led a nomadic existence, isolated from friends and began to experience fits of insanity in his twenties. In this reading the figure of the pastor who cares for the Harper relates to Johann Friedrich Oberlin, pastor of the village of Waldbach in Steinthal, in whose home in 1778 Lenz sought release from the hallucinations that were tormenting him.

sense of guilt which besets him, are subtly alluded to in the broken lines in which the Harper articulates the opening couplet (bars 6-13) and endorsed by an irregular quaver motif in the lower bass register of the piano. This prophetic image of the Harper as beggar is followed by the synecdoche in line three of the 'frommer Hand' which offers him food. The long lyrical lines of bars 14-16 acknowledge this act of charity as a pious act. Paradoxically the use of this metonymy, musically accentuated by the rising semiquaver and demisemiquaver figurations which reach into the upper registers of the treble (bars 15-16), points to the coldness of the charity, and the Harper wanders on, his movement endorsed by the recurring quaver motif (bars 17-2a) and the return of the octave motif as interlude (bars 22-24). In the second quatrain, the Harper points to his wretchedness as he relates how everyone will consider himself fortunate when they look upon him. Tears will fall down their cheeks as they gaze upon him; yet why they weep, he does not know. The image of the Harper as 'ein Bild' presents him as a sort of apparition and suggests how he stands apart from his physical self – a depiction which is musically heightened by the sparse and wide-ranging piano accompaniment of bars 25-35 a musical leitmotif of being a viewer which combines depersonalization and distance. This breakdown of individuation is supported by the closing octaves, musical designations of the wanderer and Harper, which move into the upper registers of the treble, reinforcing his isolation, as he is placed apart from his fellow men.

'Heiß mich nicht reden'

The date of 'Heiß mich nicht reden' is uncertain. Its inclusion in Goethe's *Theatralische Sendung* led scholars to place this poem before Goethe's Italian journey, with the suggested date as the autumn of 1782. Recent research has generally regarded it as a product of the nineties, while Gräf suggests a specific date as 1795. The poem was first published in *Wilhelm Meisters Lehrjahre* in 1795 and was included in Goethe's *Werke* of 1815 to 1819.[57]

In both versions of the novel 'Heiß mich nicht reden' is placed in different contexts. In the *Theatralische Sendung* it appears in Book Three, Chapter Twelve. The song is given to a minor character in Wilhelm's play, *Die königliche Einsiedlerin*, whose role is to be taken by Mignon for a future performance. Although Mignon has no acting ability, the song reflects her mental state and unhappy circumstances so vividly, that she may remain herself in adopting this role. The part offers her a release for her repressed emotions, which imbues her performance with a pathos that increases through the song. Mignon's ease in adopting this role is related in the novel:

> Eines Tages fragte das Kind, ob es seine Rolle aufsagen dürfe. Man erlaubte es ihm, und es fing folgende Stelle aus der Königlichen Einsiedlerin, die er ihr gestern abgeschrieben hatte, sehr pathetisch vorzutragen an. Er ging in der Stube hin und her, ohne sonderlich auf sie acht zu haben, indem er an etwas anders dachte

> On the day the child asked whether she could recite her role. The request was granted, and it began very poignantly reciting the part of the royal (female) hermit that he had transcribed for her the day before. He [Wilhelm] went back and forth in the room without particularly paying attention to her. He was thinking about something else

and as she recites the poem:

> Wilhelm merkte nicht auf, wie sie die ersten Verse vortrug, doch da es an die letzten kam, sprach sie solche mit einer Emphase von Innigkeit und Wahrheit aus, daß er aus seinem Traume geweckt wurde und ihm klang, als wenn ein anderer Mensch redete. Er war eben im Auf- und Abgehen weggewendet, er fuhr schnell herum, sah das Kind an, das nachdem es geendigt hatte, sich wie gewöhnlich beugte.[58]

---

[57] The only variant occurs in line nine, where 'der Freunde' is substituted for 'des Freundes'.
[58] *WA* I, 51, pp.259-60.

Wilhelm did not pay attention as she recited the first verse, however when it came to the last one she delivered it with such tenderness and truth that it awoke him from his dreams and sounded to him as if another person was speaking. As he was going back and forth he had his back to her, then swung around suddenly and looked at the child, who, when she finished, gave her customary bow.

Although Wilhelm does not know of the cause of Mignon's suffering, he realizes, as he listens to her delivery of the poem, that he has struck a hidden chord in her being. He places words in Mignon's mouth which offer her release from this distress, though paradoxically the poem relates the tragedy of a sorrow which must remain undisclosed.

In *Wilhelm Meisters Lehrjahre* Mignon's lyric is included at the end of Book Five, Chapter Sixteen. Wilhelm, we are told, is about to set out on a journey; all the necessary arrangements for his theatrical affairs have been made, and Mignon, who remains behind, bids him farewell:

> Mignon nahm den Scheidenden bei der Hand, und indem sie, auf die Zehen gehoben, ihm einen treuherzigen und lebhaften Kuß, doch ohne Zärtlichkeit, auf die Lippen drückte, sagte sie Meister! vergiß uns nicht und komm bald wieder. Und so lassen wir unsern Freund unter tausend Gedanken und Empfindungen seine Reise antreten, und zeichnen hier noch zum Schlusse ein Gedicht auf, das Mignon mit großem Ausdruck einigemal rezitiert hatte, und das wir früher mitzuteilen durch den Drang so mancher sonderbaren Ereignisse verhindert wurden. [59]

> Mignon took Wilhelm's hand, stood on tiptoe, and gave him a big, trusting kiss, but without any tenderness, saying, 'Master, don't forget us, and come back soon'. And so we leave our friend with many thoughts and feelings to set out on his journey and record at this point in our story a poem which Mignon had recited several times with great feeling and which we were prevented from communicating by the pressure of various strange incidents.

'Heiß mich nicht reden' follows and brings Book Five to a close. At first, Mignon's lyric has no obvious connection with the preceding action in this book, nor does it serve as a lead into the *Bekenntnisse einer schönen Seele* of Book Six. Yet despite its detached position, the poem reveals just enough of the mystery which surrounds Mignon to leave the reader in a state of wonder, which is perhaps the effect the poet wished to create before preceding to another theme of a mystic kind.

'Heiß mich nicht reden' is composed in three stanzas, each arranged as a quatrain. Stanza one is composed in lines of four or five beats. Line one opens with an adonic foot followed by two trochaic beats; line two follows the adonic foot with three strong beats. The second couplet is composed in iambic pentameter, with an added stress at the end of line three, followed by iambic tetrameter in line four. Goethe composes verse two in iambic pentameter, though he alters the metre of the final line to alexandrines. The change of metre highlights the contrast between the natural imagery and the secret which Mignon confesses she must retain. In the final stanza the metre returns to iambic pentameter, though the final stresses in lines ten and twelve are altered to bacchic feet. In both works Mignon recites or declaims the poem. The musicality of her lyric is enhanced by the rhyming scheme *abab cbcb dbdb* and the use of strong and weak endings. Goethe's use of end-rhyme is complemented by rich vowel sounds, which harmonize the inner lines of his poem.

The oath which Mignon speaks of in stanza three relates to a promise which she made before being rescued by Wilhelm, that she would never reveal her unhappy history. The vow was made to the Mother of God who appeared to her as she was being kidnapped. She promised to take care of Mignon and in return for this protection, the child swore a sacred oath that she would never again trust anyone, never tell her story, and would live and die in expectation of divine intervention.[60] Mignon keeps her vow, and her history is pieced together by Natalie through occasional remarks from songs and childish

---

[59] *WML* V, 16, *HA.*, 7, p.356.
[60] *WML* VIII, 3, *HA.*, 7, p.522.

indiscretions, which reveal what she intends to keep secret. At her funeral exequies the Abbé confirms her secrecy as he relates:

> Von dem Kinde, das wir hier bestatten, wissen wir wenig zu sagen. Noch ist uns unbekannt, woher es kam; seine Eltern kennen wir nicht, und die Zahl seiner Lebensjahre vermuten wir nur. Sein tiefes, verschlossenes Herz ließ uns seine innersten Angelegenheiten kaum erraten.[61]

> The child that we bury here, we know little about. We don't know where she came from nor who her parents were and we can only guess at her age. Her deep firmly locked heart gave us no inkling of what was going on inside it.

In 'Heiß mich nicht reden' Mignon's secret is a source of anxiety because of the inner burden it imposes on her. The poem expresses her perpetual inner conflict of longing to disclose her feelings and her need to hold them back. Mignon's silence is suggested as a social suppression, as she promises not to tell anyone of her incestuous past. Her aphasia reveals how human culture is bound up with linguistic rules of exchange, and the question of incest and silencing is very subtly raised. In 'Heiß mich nicht reden' Mignon's desire for confession as cure remains desire and in stanza three she maintains that only a god could release her from her vow. While her silence intrigues others, it also excludes them; it is the silence of death, and augurs her imminent demise.

Seóirse Bodley, 'Heiß mich nicht reden'

Like Prospero releasing Ariel, Mignon's voice, with its burden of loss, is released here in a modern musical setting. Following a two-bar *fortissimo* call to attention, Mignon's requests that she will not be asked to speak is rendered in fractured musical lines and a staccato accompaniment (bars 41-46, 60-65, 73-89) which endorse her aphasia and self-imposed silence as she struggles to maintain her secret. Mignon's long melismas on 'schweigen' (bars 46-48) and 'Pflicht' (bars 66-70) and pianistic gestures (bars 56, 58-59, 71-72) act as musical metaphors of release, suggesting how she would gladly unburden her heart if fate did not will her otherwise.

In stanza two Mignon's language is enriched with two poetic metaphors, which illustrate the naturalness of confidence. The beneficent results are symbolized by the circling sun which drives away darkness and bestows light in its place (bars 92-106). The outpouring of emotion is symbolized by the rock, which opens its bosom and pours its deep-hidden waters onto the earth (bars 108-123). These images of resolution and disclosure are realized in the long metaphorical lines of Bodley's second strophe which contrast with the fragmented musical expression of Mignon's secrecy voiced in the surrounding stanzas.

In the final stanza Mignon develops this theme in relation to mankind, as she relates how all men seek solace by confiding their hidden sorrows to a friend: the long melismas on 'Freund' (bars 135-39) and 'ergiessen' (bars 151-56) suggest the solace of such release. Like the outbreaks of her wildness, Mignon's partial aphasia is read in the fractured lines which recommence in bar 157, a musical reminder of her feral childhood. Her stammered avowal that only a god can release her from her silence is obscurely connected with the pathology of the traumatized child-woman who is reluctant or unable to speak of her past.

'Wer nie sein Brot mit Tränen aß'

The Harper's second song was first printed in *Wilhelm Meisters Lehrjahre* in 1795. The poem was later included in Goethe's *Werke* of 1815.[62] It is included in the *Theatralische Sendung* in Book Four, Chapter Thirteen.[63]

---

[61] *WML* VIII, 3, *HA.*, 7, p.576.

[62] The first stanza of this poem is also included in Goethe's *Maximen und Reflexionen* where he refers to the exile of Queen Louise of Prussia, as he writes:

In *Wilhelm Meisters Lehrjahre* the Harper's second song occurs in Book Two, Chapter Thirteen. Goethe introduces the lied in the opening line of this chapter, as he relates:

> In der verdrießlichen Unruhe, in der er sich befand, fiel ihm (Wilhelm) ein, den Alten aufzusuchen, durch dessen Harfe er die bösen Geister zu verscheuchen hoffte.[64]

> Wilhelm who was so restless and ill-tempered that he decided to look up the Harper in the hope that his music might dispel the evil spiritis.

Wilhelm inquires where the Harper lives and discovers that he lives in an inn, in a remote part of the town. Climbing up the stairs, he hears the sweet sounds of the harp:

> Es waren herzrührende, klagende Töne, von einem traurigen, ängstlichen Gesange begleitet. Wilhelm schlich an die Türe, und da der gute Alte eine Art von Phantasie vortrug und wenige Strophen teils singend, teils rezitierend immer wiederholte, konnte der Horcher nach einer kurzen Aufmerksamkeit ungefähr folgendes verstehen: 'Wer nie sein Brot mit Tränen aß'.[65]

> The deeply-moving, plaintive music was accompanied by anguished melancholy singing. Wilhelm crept up to the door. The old man was rhapsodising, repeating stanzas, half-singing, half-reciting, and then, after a short while, Wilhelm heard something like this: 'Wer nie sein Brot mit Tränen aß'.

The Harper's song is composed in the style of an Orphic lamentation and is an expression of his inner thoughts. The poem reflects the genre of the *planctus*. It is created in two stanzas, each containing four lines. Although the lines are mostly arranged in iambic tetrameter, this pattern is varied in both stanzas. Lines two, six and eight contain an additional unaccented beat at the end of the line; while line four is composed of two iambic and two amphibrach beats. The lines are written in alternative rhyme: *ababcdcd*.

'Wer nie sein Brot mit Tränen aß' is a song of deep despair in which the Harper has lost all hope or expectation of the happiness of love. In the novel Goethe symbolizes this through the figure of Sperata. Her name is derivative of the Italian feminine noun, *speranza*, meaning hope and she rescues the Harper from his isolation.[66] Sperata symbolizes faith uncertain, a passive anticipation of a positive future, beyond one's own control but always possible. The Harper's despair results in his loss of Hope (Sperata), without realizing that it is the product of judgements which need to be re-examined. In 'Wer nie sein Brot' the Harper confesses his dejection at love's implausibility. The opening stanza portrays his withdrawal from the world, while verse two reveals his dejection as a negative evaluation of the future, as if it were a foregone conclusion. In blaming the gods he denies responsibility for his failure; he desires love, but is utterly impotent in achieving it and he sees himself a victim of fate. The myth of an unjust and 'indifferent universe' is an excuse for inaction and stagnation, not as a method, but as conclusion.

Auch Bücher haben ihr Erlebtes, das ihnen nicht entzogen werden kann.
Wer nie sein Brot mit Tränen aß,
Wer nie die kummervollen Nächte
Auf seinem Bette weinend saß,
Der kennt euch nicht, ihr himmlischen Mächte.
Diese tiefschmerzlichen Zeilen wiederholte sich eine höchst vollkommene, angebete Königin in der grausamsten Verbannung, zu grenzenlosem Elend verwiesen. Sie befreundete sich mit dem Buche, das diese Worte und noch manche schmerzliche Erfahrung überliefert, und zog daraus einen peinlichen Trost; wer dürfte diese schon in die Ewigkeit sich erstreckende Wirkung wohl jemals verkümmern?, *MuR, HA.*, 12, pp. 494-95.

[63] The only variation in this edition is the punctuation at the end of line seven, which was originally written with a semicolon. A copy by Herder also exists. In this edition, the variants are: 'Himmelsmächte' for 'himmlischen Mächte' in line four and 'Denn' for 'Dann' in line seven.

[64] *WML* II, 13, *HA.*, 7, p.136.

[65] Ibid.

[66] In Monteverdi's opera, *Orfeo*, the librettist Striggio chooses Speranza, Hope personified, to guide Orpheus to the gates of hell.

In 'Wer nie sein Brot' the tears which flow at mealtimes, or those which are wept at night when sleep is not possible, are the result of a deep sense of remorse.[67] The guilt the Harper carries, which extends through day and night, engulfs the whole of his being and is accompanied by feelings of inadequacy and despair. In *Wilhelm Meisters Lehrjahre* this guilt is continually accentuated; in Book Four, Chapter Two the Harper tells Wilhelm:

> 'Ich bin schuldig, aber unglücklicher als schuldig.' Wilhelm hatte [...] in seinem wunderbaren Begleiter einen Menschen zu sehen geglaubt, der durch Zufall oder Schickung eine große Schuld auf sich geladen hat und nun die Erinnerung derselben immer mit sich fortschleppt.[68]

> 'I am guilty but even more unhappy than guilty.' Wilhelm believed that his strange companion was someone who had, through chance or fate, incurred some great guilt and now was continuously oppressed by the memory of it.

an opinion immediately endorsed by the Harper:

> Die Rache, die mich verfolgt, ist nicht des irdischen Richters; ich gehöre einem unerbittlichen Schicksale[69]

> The vengeance that pursues me is not that of any earthly judge; I am caught up in an inexorable fate

the source of which is revealed in Book Eight, Chapter Nine, where it is revealed that Mignon is the Harper's child by his sister, Sperata. The Harper's remorse in 'Wer nie sein Brot' results from his violation of an 'objective' moral law, and contrition has been forced on him by the 'himmlischen Mächte' which exact retribution of him. Whereas the Harper's apostrophe to the Gods points up the indifference of natural forces to human need, it also implies that guilt may be incurred by one's existence: a belief supported through the Oedipal character of his 'crime' and the presence of Mignon, who suffers a genetic attribution of guilt. Whereas 'Wer nie sein Brot' may be read as a confrontation with the divine, it is also a confrontation with the self in all its grandiose projections and painful limitations. The Harper's portrayal of the gods as a perpetual irresistible influence that controls his volitions and of the guilt that determines his conviction of damnation is a displacement of the very agonies of his identity. His demand for justice reveals the tortuous process through which the mind discovers truth in its own distortions and recognizes the limits of mortality in its own fantasies of omnipotence.

In *Maximen und Reflexionen* Goethe writes of predestination: 'Gott ist mächtiger und weiser als wir; darum macht er es mit uns nach seinem Gefallen',[70] and in 'Wer nie sein Brot mit Tränen aß' the Harper accuses the gods of such betrayal. The Harper is lonely; excluded from Paradise because of his insight into the imperfection of things. His depiction of cruelly paternal gods, who usher one into life and leave one to incur a primal guilt, expresses this bitter feeling of alienation from reality. He acknowledges his aloneness in an indifferent universe and his song may be interpreted as a rebellious rapturous assertion of inner values or an elegiac, ironical acceptance of the lack of beauty in the world. Either way, it expresses his feeling of unease in the world and the reprobation he experiences on earth. In 'Wer nie sein Brot mit Tränen aß' the Harper presents the mystery of a world order that yields up its secrets through violence. Its theme is the necessity of violence in a post-Saturnian world that leaves human life under a curse, and his song emerges as an etiological tale which portrays the themal contrast between the helplessness of man and the cruelty of the gods. The presence of the gods,

---

[67] The theme of primal guilt recurs through Goethe's works; see for example *Iphigenie*: 'Es fürchte die Götter / Das Menschengeschlecht./ Sie halten die Herrschaft /In ewigen Händen, /Und können sie brauchen /Wies ihnen gefällt', *Iphigenie* IV, v, *HA.*, 5, p.54.

[68] *WML* IV, 2, HA., 7, pp.208-09.

[69] Ibid, p.208.

[70] *MuR, HA.*, 12, p.377.

which represents a stable world order, gives the poem its tragic quality. As stanza one suggests, to violate this order is to invite suffering; the consequences are almost automatic and inevitable. This sense of inevitability connects the Harper's song with Orpheus. As in Greek tragedy, the Harper recognizes the power of divinity and the limits of his own human nature, and his song portrays this inexorability of Fate. Predestination explicitly sets out a distinction between determinate and indeterminate things – but also actions and states of affairs. In the opening stanza Goethe shows how a created will or determination follows a divine ordinance or determination, not necessarily, but freely and contingently. While the second verse depicts the gods as the true source of evil, it is clear that the Harper acquiesces in that suffering. The theme of the song is the interplay between man's control over nature and nature's destructive independence from man, where cause and motivation are both human and divine. Paradoxically, through this duality the divine essence is recognized as one single necessary and immutable cognition of all things: complexes as well as non-complexes, necessary and contingent.

Seóirse Bodley, 'Wer nie sein Brot mit Tränen aß'

Bodley's setting commences with a dramatic call to attention (bar 172) as the Harper says that he who has never eaten his bread with tears or lived through nights of anguish does not know the Heavenly powers. The Harper's opening couplet, reminiscent of Paul Gerhardt's hymn:

| Wie lange soll ich jammervoll | How long am I, full of sorrow, |
| Mein Brot mit Tränen essen[71] | To eat my bread with tears |

is plaintive in its musical expression, with Goethe's end-rhyme (lines one and three) deliberately accentuated (bars 175 and 181). The haunting lines of the Harper's recollection of nights of anguish are accompanied by a rhythmically fractured atonal counterpoint (bars 176-82), the Harper's apostrophe, 'ihr himmlischen Mächte', underscored by demi-semiquaver chords (bars 183), which magnify the intensity of these lines.

In stanza two the Harper addresses the Gods, as he imputes: 'You lead us into life, and by your will, we fall into sin' (187-191).[72] The reflective lines in which he voices this accusation and its continuance in bars 192-97, where man is delivered over to suffering, musically depict the Harper's tone of resignation. The piano accompaniment gently comments on man's fate to the closing gesture, a high D (bar 197), its *fortissimo* dissonant chord in bars 194-95 acknowledging how on earth there is retribution for every guilt.

'Kennst du das Land?'

'Kennst du das Land' is a rhythmical parody of the English ballad, 'Summer', by James Thomson in 1746.[73] The similarities between Goethe's and Thomson's lyrics have been pointed out by many scholars,[74] including Sternfield in his study, *Goethe and Music*.[75] When one compares the opening stanzas of Goethe's verse with Thomson's lyric:

---

[71] James Boyd, *Notes to Goethe's Poems* 2 vols (Oxford: Basil Blackwell, 1962), I, p.193.
[72] The idea of temptation coming from above recurs in the 'Paria Legende': 'Denn von oben kommt Verführung, / Wenn's den Gott so beliebt', *HA*, I, p.364, ll.111-12.
[73] The ballad is reprinted in *The Complete Poetical Works of James Thomson*, ed. by J. L. Robertson (London: Oxford University Press, 1908), p.78.
[74] G. von Loeper first noted this comparison in *Goethes Gedichte* 1 (Berlin: Gustav Hempel Verlag, 1882), p.353; Arthur Kutscher developed this connection in *Das Naturgefühl in Goethes Lyrik* [...] *bis 1789* (Leipzig: Breslauer Beiträge VII, 1906), pp.9 and 156.
[75] Frederick Sternfield, *Goethe and Music: A List of Parodies and Goethe's Relationship to Music: A List of References* (New York: The New York Public Library, 1979), p.34.

Bear me, Pomona! to thy citron groves;
To where the lemon and the piercing lime,
With the deep orange, glowing through the green,
Their lighter glories blend. Lay me, reclin'd,
Beneath the spreading tamarind, that shakes,
Fann'd by the breeze, its fever-cooling fruit.
                                        (lines 663-671)

the similarities are obvious. In the opening lines both poets refer to the citron groves; Goethe's image of the golden oranges which glow in the dark foliage enriches Thomson's trope in line 665, while the breeze which fans the fruit is transmuted to a soft wind which whispers from the sky. In both poems, the singer is remote from the Italian locality, to which he longs to return. Mignon's refrain, 'Dahin! Dahin Möcht' ich mit dir, o mein Gebieter, ziehn!', reflects Thomson's appeal, 'Bear me, Pomona to thy citron groves' and in both lyrics, the person they address is invested with the power to transport them there. The phrase structure in 'Kennst du das Land, wo die Zitronen blühn' reflects the original line of Thomson's 'Summer', 'Bear me, Pomona! to thy citron groves; / To where the lemon [...]', while the opening in Herder's fair copy, 'Kennst du den Ort' is closer to Thomson's image in line 663. However, while Goethe's use of language is clearly related to that of the English poet, subtle differences emerge in the opening lines of this poem. Mignon's initial question establishes a mood of solemnity, which is absent from Thomson's blithe recollection of this abode. Thomson's apostrophe is addressed to the Roman goddess, Pomona, while the identity of the person Mignon addresses remains unknown. Thomson's use of iambic pentameter is reflected in Goethe's verse and his alliteration, 'glowing through the green' (line 665), resonates in the second line of Goethe's poem, 'Im dunkeln Laub die Gold-Orangen glühn'. This influence is even more apparent in the version from the *Theatralische Sendung*, 'Im grünen Laub die Gold-Orangen glühn', where triple alliteration is employed by the poet.[76]

'Kennst du das Land' first appeared in *Wilhelm Meisters Theatralische Sendung*, in the opening chapter of the fourth book.[77] The inclusion of this poem in the first edition of this novel, which was finished in 1784, suggests that the poem was conceived before Goethe's Italian journey. Revising this manuscript as *Wilhelm Meisters Lehrjahre*, Goethe placed the poem at the beginning of Book Three. There are slight variations in these versions. Stanza one, line three originally read 'Im grünen Laub', while the refrain at the end of verse one is respectfully altered from 'Gebieter' to 'Geliebter', 'Beschützer' and 'Vater'. In addition to its inclusion in these novels, the poem was published independently with Goethe's ballads in the edition of his collected works printed in 1815.

Taken independently, Mignon's lied is deeply moving, yet its meaning and effect are both enriched when one considers it in the context of the novel. In the opening paragraphs of Book Three, Wilhelm hears music outside his door, which he assumes is the Harper, until the sound of the voice and zither accompaniment confirm that it is Mignon. When he opens the door to her, Mignon crosses the threshold and sings a song that will become her signature tune: 'Kennst du das Land'. The positioning of Mignon and her song on the threshold both in the fictional scene and in the third book is symbolic. Wilhelm is charmed by her rendition and asks her to sing it again, so that he may transcribe and translate it into German. Yet as Wilhelm discovers:

---

[76] In addition to Thomson's influence, many of the expressions and images in Goethe's verse, such as 'sanfter Wind', 'die Myrte', 'der Lorbeer'; 'das schimmern'de Gemach' and 'Höhlen und Drachen' are drawn from the Anacreontic poets.

[77] Two copies of the poem are extant: Herder's manuscript, like all his copies of the *Wilhelm Meister* poems, is without a title. Its variations are slight: 'Kennst du den Ort' (line one); 'grünen Laub' (line two); 'Gebieter' (lines seven and twenty-one); 'ihm' for 'ihn' (line nineteen). Fräulein von Göchhausen's manuscript contains 'grünen Laub' (line two) and 'Gebieter' (lines seven, fourteen and twenty-one).

die Originalität der Wendungen konnte er nur von ferne nachahmen; die kindliche Unschuld des Ausdrucks verschwand, indem die gebrochene Sprache übereinstimmend und das Unzusammenhängende verbunden ward.[78]

He found, however, that he could not even approximate the originality of the phrases, and the child-like innocence of the style was lost when the language was smoothed over and the disconnectedness removed.

Throughout the lied Mignon's memories of her childhood are set forth briefly and laconically, yet the sincerity of her diction intensifies the emotional import of the song. The enchantment of her song is enhanced by her delivery, which is described in detail as Goethe relates:

Sie fing jeden Vers feierlich und prächtig an, als ob sie auf etwas Sonderbares aufmerksam machen, als ob sie etwas Wichtiges vortragen wollte. Bei der dritten Zeile ward der Gesang dumpfer und düsterer; das 'Kennst du es wohl?' drückte sie geheimnisvoll und bedächtig aus; in dem 'Dahin! Dahin!' lag eine unwiderstehliche Sehnsucht, und ihr 'Laß uns ziehn!' wußte sie bei jeder Wiederholung dergestalt zu modifizieren, daß es bald bittend und dringend, bald treibend und vielversprechend war.[79]

She intoned each verse with a certain solemn grandeur, as if she were drawing attention to something unusual and imparting something of importance. When she reached the third line, the melody became more sombre and gloomy; the words 'do you know it, yes?' were given mystery and weight, the 'oh there, oh there!' was suffused with insatiable longing and she modified the phrase, 'Let us go', each time it was repeated, so that one time it was entreating and urging, the next time pressing and full of promise.

Mignon's lied is composed in three stanzas, each containing five lines with a two-line refrain, which is altered slightly in each verse. Goethe composes the first four lines of each stanza as a quatrain, consisting of two rhyming couplets. Like Thomson's ballad, the lines are composed in iambic pentameter, though he varies this pattern by placing the natural stress on the first syllable (line one of all three stanzas; the last line of stanzas one and two). Goethe retains the iambic feet through lines five and six, though he reduces the rhythm to two stressed beats. In line seven, he brings each verse to a close with a return to iambic pentameter, though in the first two stanzas, the first beat is varied to a trochaic foot. The rhyming scheme of each strophe is *aabbcde*. Goethe's repetition of phrases is an aesthetic, structural and rhetorical element in the poem. Each quatrain opens with the question 'Kennst du?' and is followed by the query, 'Kennst du es wohl?' This repetition enhances the musicality of each verse and lends a tight structure, while subtly pointing Mignon's change of address. Through this repetition, Mignon's questions become more urgent, while the broad vowel of the mysterious 'Vater', after the tighter vowels of 'Geliebter' and 'Beschützer', is like a cry of abandonment. As a mnemonic device common to the *Volkslied*, the refrain satisfies explicit expectations of this form, yet Goethe's artistry is recognized through this variation, which maintains the poetic tension through each refrain.

Ostensibly 'Kennst du das Land' expresses Mignon's longing for her homeland, Italy. The location which Mignon describes is uncertain as she herself cannot reveal its identity. The flora, the architecture and journey through the Alps suggest Italy. An exact location is given in Goethe's *Wanderjahre* where Mignon's childhood scenes are placed by Lake Maggiore, while the district of Vicenza is referred to as her home in the *Italienische Reise*. In 'Kennst du das Land' Mignon's recollection of Italy, with its blossoms and fruits, kindles her nostalgia, as she longs for the colour and warmth of the scenes of her youth. Although the memories of her childhood are vague, her longing for her homeland is intense, and it recurs as a motif throughout the novel. In Book Five, Chapter Two she studies some maps with Felix, yet her interest lies not in the location of countries, but in

---

[78] *WML* III, 1, *HA.*, 7, p.146.
[79] Ibid.

their climate.[80] In Book Five, Chapter Sixteen, Wilhelm sets out on a journey. When Mignon asks him whether he is going south or north and he tells her it is the latter, she declines accompanying him. Mignon's desire for her homeland reflects Goethe's personal longing for Italy, whose attraction to this Italian milieu is found in fragments for a Homeric drama, a tragedy of *Nausikaa*, whose description of the southern country echoes the opening imagery of 'Kennst du das Land':

Dort dringen neben Früchten wieder Blüten,	There beside the fruit new flowers blossom
Und Frucht auf Früchte wechseln durch das Jahr.	And there is a constant exchange of fruit through the year.
Die Pomeranze, die Zitrone steht	The pomegranates, the lemons stand,
Im dunklen Laube, und die Feige folgt	In dark foliage, and figs
Der Feige.[81]	Follow figs.

Later in the *Italienische Reise* he relates how the climate, the blue southern sky and the lush vegetation of the Mediterranean landscape afforded him daily delight and in the *Römische Elegien* (VII) he complains of the grey sky, the colourless and formless world of the north.[82] While Goethe's inclusion of 'Kennst du das Land' in the *Theatralische Sendung* reveals the maturity of his vision of the classical world before his flight to Italy, it also confesses his desire to see it with his own eyes. Conversely, the vague kind of nostalgia which is expressed in 'Kennst du das Land', is not specifically for the country, nor for any particular place or person, but for all that Italy seemed to symbolize, for all that is brighter and nobler than actuality.

In 'Kennst du das Land' Mignon's longing is for the lost Heaven which lay around her in infancy. The sunny climate and blue skies symbolize the happy days of Mignon's youth. Her journey through the Alps is symbolic of the transition from childhood, the passing of time, yet, paradoxically, the pathway leads back to the past. Mignon's desire to return to her childhood symbolizes an especial need for tenderness and protection, which is suggested through her address to Wilhelm as father and protector. Her desire to recover her childhood expresses the desire to recover the intense nurturance of early infancy. In addressing Wilhelm as father, she seeks to rediscover the relationship which was most meaningful to her in childhood, and her relationship to him is characterized by a strong dependence on him. In Book Eight, Chapter Nine, the Marchese's memory of Mignon's country childhood suggests how she was once self-contained and recalls her as a symbol of natural simplicity and spontaneity. In 'Kennst du das Land' Mignon's desire to recapture this childhood seeks a return to lost innocence; a return to this paradisiacal state. The location of her childhood is given the traditional depiction of paradise as a garden luxuriating in plants and trees. As an image of Earthly Paradise it contains rich soil and a pleasant climate, but with the suggestion of eternal daylight and perpetual spring. Mignon's memories of childhood correlate to the mythic realm of Thule in *Faust*, a spiritual centre, which is identified with the desire to regain peace and perfection. Her loss of this paradise and her desire to return to it suggest how she knows no more peace, and her search for a lost paradise is an expression of her feelings of abandonment.

In 'Kennst du das Land' Goethe explores the theme of cultural filialogy, and the poem may be read as an allegory of the relationship between women and the outer world of cultural power. Here culture implies the structures of meaning through which people give shape to their experience and in this lyric Goethe examines the absence of a father in Mignon's cultural development. In literary, mythic and historical texts of parent-child relationships the father and son are the first pair most frequently in focus; mother-son

---

[80] *WML* V,1, *HA.*, 7, p.283.
[81] *Nausikaa*, I, iii, *HA.*, 5, p.71.
[82] *Italienische Reise*, *HA.*, 1, p.162.

the next, while until recent years the narrative of father and daughter remained wrapped in invisibility. In 'Kennst du das Land' Goethe examines the psycho-social implications of the father-daughter dynamic. Mignon is the Harper's daughter, yet being the Harper's daughter is a symbolic position rather than an actual relationship. The father has abandoned her by desertion and remoteness, and his absence has shaped her destiny. The story of abandoned daughters in search of their fathers is one of the most ancient in mythology and in 'Kennst du das Land' the dialectic of lost father and yearning daughter is explored.

In 'Kennst du das Land' the theme of paternal neglect serves as a suggestive hieroglyph that masks the seemingly opposite impetus of transgressive desire. In *Wilhelm Meisters Lehrjahre* the relation to the Oedipus myth is developed where Mignon takes the part of Antigone, while Wilhelm takes the place of her father.[83] It is him she witnesses in his 'blindness'; him she leads to Natalie and with her demise Wilhelm gains insight. Mignon's Oedipal identification with Wilhelm is unveiled in this poem as she addresses him as both lover and father. Her apostrophe to the father, absent and mysterious, is a symbolic expression of incestuous wishes and at the same time an unconscious repression of this desire.[84] Underlying the narration of daughter abandonment in 'Kennst du das Land' is a text of unconscious incestuous longing, one that is born to the daughter and one that is structurally reflected in the emblematically conjunctive death of her mother, Sperata. As in her relationship to Wilhelm, the Harper's relationship to Mignon may be read as a variation of the myth of Oedipus and Antigone, with Mignon as loyal daughter who leads her father in the blinded exile to which his incestuous marriage with his sister has condemned him.[85]

Seóirse Bodley, 'Kennst du das Land?'

Bodley's 'Kennst du das Land?' points towards an untold story of Mignon's homeland, her origins and her abduction. In contrast to his musical predecessors, Bodley's setting is less preoccupied with the sunny world that she longs for than with the anguish she implies. His musical portrayal of arrest at a threshold is announced in the five-bar pianistic gesture of repeated thirds, A flat and C, which introduce Mignon's signature tune and underscore her opening words (bars 198-202). This recurring gesture which frames the long lyrical lines in which Bodley scores Mignon's scenes of childhood and the increasing urgency of her refrain subtly observe her song's strophic structure in a modern atonal setting. The evocative lines of Mignon's first scene portray a paradisiacal Mediterranean scene, where lemon and orange trees blossom,[86] myrtle and bay trees are unruffled by a wind which blows from a blue sky (bars 200-13). Yet the distinctive atonality in which Bodley expresses this scene is as unsettling as Mignon's refrain, which softly addresses her question to her beloved 'Kennst du es wohl?' (bars 214-5) before a rising musical

---

[83] In this analysis I specifically interpret Mignon in relation to the Oedipus myth rather than in relation to the Electra Complex, which does not relate as closely to Mignon's plight.

[84] Conversely, as 'Kennst du das Land' links Mignon's awakening soul to love with the filial fantasy of paternal seduction, the seduction may be read as fantasy, a product and expression of Mignon's emerging sexuality, rather than of the power and desires of the father.

[85] This relation to the Oedipus myth is also suggested in Goethe's novel where the Harper fears Mignon wishes to kill him until he realizes she is a girl, *WML*, VII, 4, HA., 7, p.437.

[86] The scene of Mignon's childhood corresponds to the scene of the Harper's affair with Sperata, where he asks the Marchese: 'Begegnet uns unter jenen Zypressen, die ihre ernsthaften Gipfel gen Himmel wenden, besucht uns an jenen Spalieren, wo die Zitronen und Pomeranzen nebens uns blühn, wo die zierliche Myrte uns ihre zarten Blumen darreicht' (Come and meet us beneath those cypresses that extend gravely into the sky, visit us in those groves where lemons and pomegranates surround us, and the tender myrtle unfolds its delicate blossoms – and then try to frighten us with your dismal, gray, man-made entrapments), *WML*, VIII, 9, *HA*., 7, p.583. Through this relation, the Harper's fate is linked with Mignon's in her opening song. The image of the laurel tree in 'Kennst du das Land' may also subtly allude to this connection, for in Greek mythology it is associated with the figure of the harper and is a symbol of hidden knowledge.

gesture (bar 215) and *piu mosso* chords (bars 216-17) affirm her desire to revisit that land with him: a transposed musical gesture of arrest, F sharp and A, ironically underscoring her words (bars 218-21).

This musical gesture drops down a third to D and F for stanza two over which a new question is raised. Here Mignon enquires whether her beloved knows the palatial home where she once lived. Again Bodley underscores her description of the villa she frequented as a child in long lyrical atonal lines which describe how its roof rests on columns, its hall and chambers glitter, and marble figures stand within its walls, the uneasy splendour of the scene underscored by atonal counterpoint (bars 225-31). Bodley's performance direction 'stonily' (bar 233-36) musically accentuates the coldness of these figures, which highlights the lack of human care she has received. As they look down at Mignon and ask 'Was hat man dir, du armes Kind, getan?' (what have they done to you, poor child?), the octaves which underscored the Harper's anguish in 'An die Türen' now return to raise their question: a subtle allusion to the pathological effects of severance and abuse. Although their question remains unanswered and the mystery of her past is retained, the urgency in which Mignon states the rising lines of her refrain (bar 239-39) suggests how she longs for a homeland that is elsewhere. Once again the notion of arrest is suggested through the vocal line where 'ziehen' is deliberately held back in its musical expression, and the musical gesture of arrest, A and C, returns (bars 241-42).

In stanza two Mignon ponders on her unhappy fate and in verse three, she alludes to this misfortune as she describes the mountainous journey which she made through the Alps. Here Bodley's gesture of arrest is musically transformed into a journeying motif which underscores Mignon's uneasy memory of a pathway shrouded with the clouds, a mule making his way through this mist, and mountain caves harbouring an ancient brood of dragons (bars 244-53). With the semiquaver gesture depicting a stream rushing over the rock-face her journey hurtles to a close. As Mignon repeats her question, 'Kennst du ihn wohl?', now addressing her lover as father, the musical gesture of arrest returns (bar 260) as she longs to venture there with him once more. The soaring thirds in the treble, voiced *sempre diminuendo*, render her answer in musical form.

'Wer sich der Einsamkeit ergibt'

The date of 'Wer sich der Einsamkeit ergibt' is uncertain. The lyric appears in Book Four of the *Theatralische Sendung*,[87] which was finished in 1783 and fixes the date *ad quem*. The poem was first published in *Wilhelm Meisters Lehrjahre* in 1795 and was reprinted in Goethe's collected works of 1815.

The Harper's third song also appears in Book Two, Chapter Thirteen, almost immediately after the Harper's rendition of 'Wer nie sein Brot mit Tränen aß'. Wilhelm sits beside the Harper on the edge of his straw bed and beseeches him:

> Singe mir, was du willst, was zu deiner Lage paßt, und tue nur, als ob ich gar nicht hier wäre. Es scheint mir, als ob du heute nicht irren könntest. Ich finde dich sehr glücklich, daß du dich in der Einsamkeit so angenehm beschäftigen und unterhalten kannst, und, da du überall ein Fremdling bist, in deinem Herzen die angenehmste Bekanntschaft findest.[88]

> Sing me whatever you have a mind to, whatever you're in a mood for – and pretend I'm not here. It seems to me that today nothing can go wrong for you. I think you are very fortunate to be able to occupy yourself so pleasantly in your solitude, and, since you are everywhere a stranger, to enjoy the intimacy of your own heart.

---

[87] In this edition, 'dann' is printed for 'erst' in line fourteen. In Herder's manuscript 'mich' is used for 'bei' in line eleven and 'denn' is used in lieu of 'erst' in line fourteen.

[88] *WML* II, 13, HA., 7, p.137.

With this the musician looks down at the strings of his harp, his fingers gliding softly over them and sings 'Wer sich der Einsamkeit ergibt'. Following the song, Wilhelm engages in conversation with the Harper, and theme of musical communication emerges through the narrator's remark:

> Auf alles, was der Jüngling zu ihm sagte, antwortete der Alte mit der reinsten Übereinstimmung durch Anklänge, die alle verwandten Empfindungen rege machten und der Einbildungskraft ein weites Feld eröffneten.[89]

> The old man responded, as though agreeing with everything the young man said, by producing music that evoked all sorts of similar feelings and opened up a broad horizon for the imagination.

The chapter closes with a comparison of the Harper's lieder to Pietist hymns. The passage suggests the element of parody and improvisation in his songs,[90] while the effect which the music has on the listener is reinforced.[91]

Goethe's lyric is composed in two stanzas each containing eight lines.[92] The first strophe is composed of two quatrains, while verse two divides the stanza into five and three. The metre is varied through the poem and the breakdown of rhythm anticipates the poet's mental state. In the first quatrain, lines one and three are composed in iambic tetrameter, with lines two and four created in iambic trimeter. In the second quatrain lines five and eight are written in iambic trimeter, line six contains two bacchic feet, while line seven is composed in iambic dimeter. In the second strophe the metre is much freer: line nine is written as an iamb, followed by a bacchic and two iambic feet; line ten contains an iamb, a bacchic and an iambic beat; line eleven is written in iambic tetrameter. In the second strophe lines twelve to fourteen and line sixteen are written in iambic trimeter. Line fifteen, 'Einsam im Grabe sein' is altered to a bacchic foot, followed by two iambic beats. In 'Wer sich der Einsamkeit ergibt' the musical quality of the poem is achieved partly through the rhyming scheme, *abcbddbb ebebddbb*, where both stanzas share a common pattern and rhyme. The musicality of the lyric is linked with the development of the theme, where the repetition of 'allein', 'Pein', 'einsam' and 'Einsamkeit' accentuate the Harper's isolation through his song. By concluding with the end rhyme 'sein' and 'allein', the lyric closes with a strong sense of the Harper's pain. The musicality of 'Wer sich der Einsamkeit ergibt' is enhanced by Goethe's assonance, where the dipthong *ei* from this end-rhyme runs through each line of the poem. This use of internal rhyme appears in the opening stanza in 'Einsamkeit', 'allein', 'ein', 'ein', 'seiner' 'Pein'; 'meiner', 'einmal', 'einsam' and 'allein'. In verse two it reappears in 'schleicht', 'seine', 'überschleicht', 'Einsamen' (line twelve and thirteen), 'einmal', 'einsam', 'sein' and 'allein'. In addition the vowel a runs in counterpoint in verse one: 'allein', 'laßt', 'Qual', 'kann', 'einmal', 'einsam', 'dann' and is repeated in the second strophe through: 'sacht', 'allein', 'Tag' 'Nacht', 'Einsamen' 'einmal', 'einsam' and 'allein'. The musical effect is further enhanced through the direct repetition of 'einsam' ('Einsamkeit'; 'Einsamen'), 'einmal', 'allein', 'schleicht' (and 'überschleicht') which runs through both stanzas. Through this use of rhyme and repetition, Goethe creates a lonely and melancholic mood. The tone is contemplative and sorrowful.

In the classical myth, Orpheus's most famous song is of love and death, of love-in-death, of death invading the happiness of love, and the idea that not even Orpheus's song

---

[89] Ibid, p.138.

[90] Although Sternfield does not relate this lyric to any one source, he recognizes it as: 'an articulate exposition of parody and improvisation' and relates it to hymns of the Herrnhut community through the passage in Goethe's *Lehrjahre, Goethe and Music: A List of Parodies*, p.79.

[91] *WML* II, 13, *HA.*, 7, pp.136-37.

[92] In *WML* the poem is arranged into two stanzas. In the *Theatralische Sendung* and in Goethe's *Werke* of 1815, the first verse is divided into two stanzas, each containing four lines. A further copy by Herder arranges the poem in four separate quatrains, yet as Loeper points out: 'die Abschnitte sind nicht sicher erkennbar'. Reprinted in Boyd, *Notes to Goethe's Poems*, I, p.170.

could reverse death has become the rhetorical topos of consolation literature. In 'Wer sich der Einsamkeit ergibt' the woman the Harper desires is not the visible Sperata of daylight, but the invisible, mysterious Other, whose primary attraction is the fullness of death living in her.[93] The poem portrays the irresistible power of death and the Harper's helplessness before it. Whereas this attraction to death is traditionally interpreted in relation to Romanticism, the Harper's extreme sensitivity to the otherness of things is not portrayed as a positive quality. In 'Wer sich der Einsamkeit ergibt' the Harper's intersubjective exchange with the life of nature threatens the boundaries of the self and his intensity places him at the edge of the abyss of terrible loss. The threat that Goethe's Harper faces is not so much death *per se* as the meaninglessness that death symbolizes: the depths of Negation in the human soul and in the world order. The song suggests how no hell is more terrifying than that of one's own inner darkness: this is the Hades the Harper cannot defeat. The poem dramatizes the artist's risk in descending into the abyss of his own soul, knowing that imaginative art creates largely *ex nihilo*.

Seóirse Bodley, 'Wer sich der Einsamkeit ergibt'

The contemplation of a fundamental truth that he who turns to solitude soon finds himself alone is announced by the Harper's *piano* accompanying chords (bars 270-71), the harper's isolation endorsed by the sparse accompaniment in the higher registers of the piano. As is characteristic of this setting, Bodley highlights the poet's repetition of the dipthong 'ei' here through a syncopated setting of Goethe's endrhyme, 'allein' (bar 275). The poet develops this idea in the second couplet: where everyone is concerned with his own life and love, 'lebt' and 'liebt' subtly pointed (bars 276 and 279), leaving the Harper to suffer alone, his musical line tailing off on 'Pein' (bars 283-84). Another suggestive spread chord heralds the Harper's passionate outcry to leave him to his pain (bars 285-87). Paradoxically, he recognizes that, if he dwells in solitude, he will never be alone; Bodley's characteristic pointing of 'allein' in bars 293-94, reminding us that the Harper's sorrow is ever with him and there is no escape.

Once again Bodley heralds stanza two with a *piano* harp chord (bars 295-96). The verse opens with the image of a lover who stealthily goes to discover whether his beloved is alone, the high F sharp, marked falsetto, again highlighting the Harper's repetition of 'allein'.[94] Here in stanza two the clandestine nature of the lover's visit is accompanied by a sparse atonal counterpoint (bars 297-310). The Harper's sorrow is endorsed against a wide-ranging melody (see, for example bar 304), by rising lines leading to 'Qual' (bars 308-10), a sustained *forte* dissonant chord (bars 311-313), and a recitative-like setting of the image of the grave. In the descending lines which affirm how only in the grave he is really alone (bars 311-18), 'allein' is again vocally accentuated (bars 318-18); the piano momentarily disappears leaving the Harper to face the terrors of his own soul. This musical depiction is subtly suggested in the sparse layout of the *pianissimo* postlude which affirms how only death can offer release.

'So laßt mich scheinen bis ich werde'

Mignon's final song is not included in the *Theatralische Sendung*. In *Wilhelm Meisters Lehrjahre* it appears in Book Eight, Chapter Two. At a birthday party, Mignon is dressed as an angel in a long white robe, fastened with a golden belt and wearing a diadem of gold. In one hand she carries a lily and in the other she carries a basket of presents, which she distributes to the children. As she enters, Natalie announces, 'Da kommt ein Engel'.

---

93 This anology is drawn from Goethe's novel where Sperata is referred to as the Bride of Death. Her death gives her a kind of second virginity in which she is unreachable, untouchable, which is characteristic of the Maiden wedded to Death, *WML* VIII, 9, *HA.*, 7, pp. 586-89 and p.591.

94 In line nine, the word 'sacht' (softly) is of North German origin, the poetic equivalent of its cognate 'sanft'.

At first the children withdraw and then, recognizing her, cry out 'Es ist Mignon'. Yet they are seized by a strange feeling that she may somehow really be an angel and are reluctant to approach her. As Mignon distributes the presents, the children gather around her in amazement. One of the children asks, 'Bist du ein Engel?' (Are you an Angel) to which Mignon replies, 'Ich wollte, ich wär es' (I wish I were). They inquire why she carries a lily, and Mignon explains: 'So rein und offen sollte mein Herz sein, dann wär' ich glücklich' (My heart should be open and pure as a lily, then I would be happy),[95] while her wings 'stellen schönere vor, die noch nicht entfaltet sind' (stand for lovelier wings which are not yet opened). When the children's curiosity is satisfied, they want to undress her, yet Mignon is loath to change back into her earthly attire. She asks that she remain in costume for a while, until at last she is in reality what she appears to be. Her song, which she accompanies on the zither, expresses not merely her fervent wish to retain her costume, but also the revelation that, young as she is, she is soon to leave this life and assume the role of an angel for which she feels destined.

Mignon's song is composed in four quatrains. Each stanza is composed in iambic tetrameter, with the first and third lines containing an extra beat. The poem is composed in alternative rhyme: *abab cdcd efef ghgh*. The musicality of the poem is enhanced through assonance: for example: 'scheinen' and 'weiße' (verse one), 'kleine' and 'reine' (verse two), and alliteration: 'keine Kleider' (verse three), 'Sorg' and 'Schmerz' (stanza four).

In 'So laßt mich scheinen' Mignon's adoption of angelic robes is symbolic of her underlying character. Goethe develops this motif through the novel where her clothes are the external symbols of spiritual potency, an expression of the essential truth of her character, revealing the changing aspects of her personality. In Book Two, Chapter Four, Mignon's boyish attire reflects her membership of the acrobatic troupe, while her change of dress into Wilhelm's colours indicates her sense of belonging with him. In casting off this apparel she denies her connections with him, as she is invested in angelic robes. In 'So laßt mich scheinen' Mignon's adoption of this clothing introduces her sacralization in the final book. Her first appearance as an angel is made in relation to this song and, following the pageant, she remains dressed in similar robes. In Book Eight, Chapter Two, Natalie alludes to Mignon's preternatural appearance when she first adopts her angelic robes.[96] When Wilhelm returns from his travels, he finds her dressed 'im langen weißen Frauengewande' (in a long white dress).[97] Following her death he refers to her as 'den abgeschiedenen Engel' (the departed angel),[98] and during her funeral exequies in Book Eight, Chapter Eight, the child 'lag in seinen Engelkleidern, wie schlafend, in der angenehmsten Stellung' (lay in its angel costume sleeping, in a most pleasing posture).[99] In Book Eight, Chapter Nine as the Marchese relates her ancestry, it is revealed that Sperata received a vision of her child as an angel before her death.[100] In 'So laßt mich scheinen' Goethe adopts the symbol of dress in its most highly worked Gnostic guise, as an emblem of the very essence of Mignon's being. By transmission of a robe, she signifies

---

[95] The symbolism of the lily is also given in the Marchese's account of his brother's past. In defence of his relationship with Sperata, the Harper refers to this flower as he relates: 'Seht die Lilien an: entspringt nicht Gatte und Gattin auf einem Stengel? Verbindet beide nicht die Blume, die beide gebar, und ist die Lilie nicht das Bild der Unschuld, und ist ihre geschwisterliche Vereinigung nicht fruchtbar?' (Consider the lilies: Do not husband and wife grow on one and the same stem? Does not the flower that bore both unite them? And is not the lily the image of innocence? Is not its sibling union fruitful?, *WML* VIII, 9, *H.A.*, 7, p.584. As noted in the introduction, the white lily is traditionally associated with the hermaphrodite; it is the attribute of many deities and in Christian iconography it is connected with the Divine Mother, to whom Mignon, like Gretchen, turns for solace.

[96] *WML* VIII, 2, *HA.*, 7, p.516.

[97] ibid., p.525.

[98] ibid., p.545.

[99] ibid., p.577.

[100] ibid., p.591.

putting off the old self and adopting the new persona. The ritual changing of Mignon's garment marks her passage from one world to another and her angelic dress signifies her withdrawal from the world. It not only indicates the ephemeral nature of her life as indicated in stanza one, but signifies her inner detachment from the present and attachment to distant and higher ends.

To Mignon, Goethe imputes the same insight, the same prophetic preternatural character as the androgynous Greek gods. As in Classical mythology, Mignon's intuition is irrational and her powers of Unreason grant her a knowledge of ultimate and fundamental truths. Her clairvoyant powers represent, in some way, the pristine undivided unity at the very root of herself, almost uncreative in its aloofness from the conflicts and contradictions of living. As in 'Kennst du das Land', it is linked to that part of man which knows best the paradisiacal region, where Mignon feels at one with herself. The portrayal of Mignon as prophetess is first evident in Book Seven, Chapter Eight, where Mignon reveals that she had divined that Felix was Wilhelm's son.[101] And in 'So laßt mich scheinen' Mignon's adoption of angelic clothes anticipates her future destiny. In both cases Mignon's intuition is not based on 'Reality'; it is direct knowledge that she cannot support with any *logos*, yet the immediacy of her knowledge is continually affirmed in the literary context. As the angelic state is linked with the prophetic state, knowledge of her impending death serves Mignon provisionally as premises and it is from this basis that she can go forward.

Seóirse Bodley, 'So laßt mich scheinen bis ich werde'

As the eight books of *Wilhelm Meisters Lehrjahre* were composed one after another between 1794-96, Goethe sent them to Schiller, who read them enthusiastically and critically and recorded his impressions in his correspondence with Goethe. As Schiller records in his letter to Goethe of 28 June 1976, one of Mignon's songs leaps off the page:

> Aus der Masse der Eindrücke, die ich empfangen, ragt mir in diesem Augenblick Mignons Bild am stärksten hervor. Ob die so stark interessierte Empfindung hier noch mehr fordert, als ihr gegeben worden, weiß ich jetzt noch nicht zu sagen. Es könnte auch zufällig sein; denn beim Aufschlagen des Manuskriptes fiel mein Blick zuerst auf das Lied, und dies bewegte mich so tief, daß ich den Eindruck nachher nicht mehr auslöschen konnte.[102]

> Out of the mass of impressions that I received, the image of Mignon rises up most powerfully before me at this moment. Whether the strength of feeling engaged on her behalf demands still more than has in fact been given to her, I cannot yet say. It might also be an accident: for when I opened the manuscript, the first thing that caught my eye was the song, and that moved me so deeply that I found myself subsequently no longer able to erase that impression.

The song in question was 'So laßt mich scheinen', a scene in which Mignon is an earthly embodiment of an angelic hermaphrodite, expressive of opposites, fused together and integrated into Oneness.[103] As a result of the dynamic tendencies of these contradictions (male and female, unity and division, earthly and divine), and through her link with the phenomenal world, Mignon represents a system of perpetual inversions. In 'So laßt mich scheinen' Bodley symbolizes the transformation of Mignon's being into another through a musical symbolism of Inversion, the opening line of her song (bars

---

[101] *WML* VII, 8, *HA.*,7, p.473.

[102] For the chronology of Goethe's correspondence with Schiller during the completion and publication of the Lehrjahre, see Nicholas Boyle, *Goethe: The Poet and the Age*, vol.2, *Revolution and Renunciation* (1790-1803) (Oxford: Oxford University Press, 2000), pp.233 and 405.

[103] In a letter to Goethe on 2 July 1796, Schiller alludes to this quality in Mignon and the Harper, when he writes of the design of *Wilhelm Meister*: 'Es steht da wie ein schönes Planetsystem, alles gehört zusammen, und nur die italienischen Figuren knüpfen, wie Kometengestalten und auch so schauerlich wie diese, das System an ein Enferntes und Größeres an' (*Briefe an Goethe*, 2, *Von Schiller*, Letter no.161, 2 July 1796, p.233).

328-333), a retrograde inversion four, in which the four moveable notes are voiced enharmonically:

Musical Example 2: Bodley, 'So laßt mich scheinen', retrograde inversion 4

Bodley's accompaniment figuration oscillates between its opening gestures of transformation (bars 325-28) and recurring thirds gesture, which in her signature tune once was a musical symbol of arrest. In stanza one Mignon requests that she may retain her angelic appearance. Bodley's vocal melismas on 'werde' (stanza one, bars 331-33), '(weisse) Kleid' (stanza one, bars 336-37), 'verklärten (Leib)' (stanza three, bars 375-77), 'wieder jung' (bars 393-98) underscore her impending death and transfiguration. Mignon's angelic transformation (bars 338-40) and traditional portrayal of the grave as a house and changeless abode (bars 344-45, 346-49) herald a return of the thirds motif which prepares the opening line of stanza two, 'dort ruh ich eine kleine Stille' before she is transformed in death. Her transfiguration in stanza two and three in which she will leave behind her pure chrysalis, her garments and her wreath, is subtly underscored by this motif (bars 358-65, 367-70, 373, 375). Bodley's opening gestures of transformation herald the paradoxes of the final stanza in which Mignon recounts how she has lived without care or trouble, though she has borne deep sorrow in the past, an experience that has aged her prematurely and which signals her request that she may be eternally reborn.

'Nur wer die Sehnsucht kennt'

The date of 'Nur wer die Sehnsucht kennt' is more precise than most of the *Wilhelm Meister Lehrjahre* poems. In a letter to Charlotte von Stein on 20 June 1785, Goethe enclosed a copy of the lyric, with the note: 'Hierbei ein Liedchen von Mignon aus dem sechsten Buche, ein Lied, das nun auch mein ist' (enclosed a little song of Mignon's from the sixth book, a song that is also mine),[104] while his letter on 27 June 1785, ends with the title words of the poem.[105]

In *Wilhelm Meisters Lehrjahre*, the lied, 'Nur wer die Sehnsucht kennt', is introduced at the end of Book Four, Chapter Eleven. The song is introduced in relation to Wilhelm, who lapses into a dreamy longing:

> und wie einstimmend mit seinen Empfindungen war das Lied, das eben in dieser Stunde Mignon und der Harfner, als ein unregelmäßiges Duett mit dem herzlichsten Ausdrucke sangen: 'Nur wer die Sehnsucht kennt'.[106]

> And the passionate expressiveness of the free duet that Mignon and the Harper were singing, was like an echo of what he himself was feeling: 'Nur wer die Sehnsucht kennt'.

In the *Theatralische Sendung* it appears at the end of Book Six, Chapter Six, where it is sung as a solo by Mignon, with harp accompaniment. Again, it is introduced in an indirect manner:

> Er [Wilhelm] hing den süßen Vorstellungen nach, und ein Verlangen bemächtigte sich seiner, das er nie in seinem Busen gefühlt. Mignon und der Alte hatten schon eine Weile

[104] *WA* IV, 7, Letter no.2139, *An Charlotte von Stein*, 20 June 1785, p.67.
[105] *Goethe Briefe*, 1, *HA*, Letter no. 380, *An Charlotte von Stein*, 27 June 1785, p.480.
[106] *WML* IV, 11, *HA*., 7, p.240.

in dem Nebenzimmer zur Harfe gesungen, endlich machte eine unbekannte Melodie unsern Freund aufmerksam, er horchte, Mignon sang: 'Nur wer die Sehnsucht kennt'.[107]

[Wilhelm] surrendered to the sweet image, and a longing seized him which he had never experienced before. Mignon and the old man had already been singing to the accompaniment of the harp for quite a while in the other room; finally an unknown melody caught our friend's attention and he listened as Mignon sang 'Nur wer die Sehnsucht kennt'.

In 'Nur wer die Sehnsucht kennt' Mignon's unwavering desire is expressed in a single strophe. Her song contains twelve lines, which are freely composed. The lyric is arranged as a sestet, followed by two couplets and a restatement of lines one and two, which acts as a refrain. Although the poem is not created with a strict metre, the lines alternate between two and three beats, iambic and trochaic feet, closing with alternating masculine and feminine cadences. The lyric is arranged in alternative rhyme, *ababacacabab*, where the rhyme *c* echoes *b*. Through this use of rhyme, the lyric is composed as a monostrophe, where the thematic movement of the poem is reflected through Goethe's use of end-rhyme. The refrain (lines one and two) forms the frame, the lament; lines three to four, nine to ten convey Mignon's inner state (*ab*), while the middle quatrain implies a movement away from the speaker (*ac*). As with this end-rhyme, Goethe's use of assonance and alliteration enhances the musicality of Mignon's song. In line two 'weiß' and 'leide' link with 'allein' in line three, while 'Freude' connects with 'Firmament' in lines four and five.

In analysis of this poem, many musicologists define *Sehnsucht* in terms of Romantic longing. Reed considers the song 'is best regarded as an expression of that generalized feeling of nostalgia which belonged both to the characters in the story and to the age in which they lived',[108] and Flothuis considers it 'is the psychic motive of early romanticism' which 'cannot be translated in one word. It includes the notions of: longing for something unattainable; realizing the fact that what is wanted, is unattainable; self-indulgence, revelling in this feeling, in this idea'.[109] Yet Goethe's conception of *Sehnsucht* is not used with the same Romantic connotations. The German word for yearning, *Sehnsucht*, has itself, and particularly in Goethe's usage, an incandescent physical quality about it. It is the function of man's whole being in its highest exaltation: a spiritual link between existence and the essence of beings.[110] In 'Nur wer die Sehnsucht kennt' Mignon's passion is portrayed as a distinctly human experience: entirely natural and exceedingly intense. As in 'Gretchen am Spinnrade' desire is revealed as something deeply active within the human heart, and Mignon's awareness and experience of it stymie all attempts to rest content. In both songs Goethe recognizes the unity between passion and suffering, whereby 'Sehnsucht' carries its religious connotations and passionate love is portrayed as a gift that assumes total suffering and loss.[111] This portrayal of love as wound is a frequent theme with Goethe: in 'Nur wer die Sehnsucht kennt' Mignon loves and suffers for what she loves.

The subject of exile has a lengthy historical and mythical dimension: the exile of Adam and Eve from the Garden of Eden, the wanderings of Odysseus and Orpheus, the labyrinthine disorientation in Goethe's protagonists all speak to a fundamental sense of loss, of displacement and a desire to regain a paradisiacal sense of unity and wholeness. In 'Nur wer die Sehnsucht kennt' this essence of exile lies at the heart of Goethe's poem in

---

[107] *WA* I, 52, p.225.

[108] John Reed, *The Schubert Song Companion* (Manchester: Manchester University Press, 1985), p.347.

[109] Marius Flothuis, 'Franz Schubert's Compositions to Poems from Goethe's *Wilhelm Meister Lehrjahre*' in *Notes on Notes: Selected Essays* (Amsterdam, F. Knuf, 1974), p.126.

[110] See for example Goethe's lyrics 'Auf dem See' or 'Rastlose Liebe' where love is continually linked with Nature.

[111] The spiritual significance of Mignon's passion is suggested through the appearance of the cross on her arms, *WML* VIII, 8, *HA.*, p.577.

which exile is portrayed as one of the saddest of fates. Whether, like the Harper, the exile is isolated through social transgressions or is nostalgic like Mignon, who experiences the most unnerving form of exile: exile in the home – when that which should be the safest, most intimate, becomes alien and restless – Goethe suggests how an exile is inconsolable, forever shadowed by an absence of stability. Through Mignon, Goethe shows how exile involves dislocation on several levels. There is physical dislocation, cultural exile and the linguistic exile of functioning in another language. In the *Theatralische Sendung*, Mignon's pronominal switches between the first and the third person reflecting the heroine's alienated perspective, and in the *Lehrjahre* Goethe shows the difficulty Mignon experiences in negotiating an identity for herself. As in 'Kennst du das Land?' Mignon's duet presents us with a double sense of exile: exile from a lost youth and from a lost culture, which reveals a series of other borders that are metaphysical in nature, and asks questions about identity and meaning that are characteristic of late twentieth-century culture.

So too the Harper's life in exile as one season succeeds another contrasts to Virgil's seven months and Ovid's three years. In *Wilhelm Meisters Lehrjahre* Goethe's Harper demonstrates the poet's interest in the doctrinal and philosophical implications of the myth, as well as its purely narrative aspect. In Goethe's Harper his 'backward glance' is fixed and he is trapped in a fallen time (a fall of hope rather than a fall into despair): what he desires in this duet is neither present nor possible within himself. He longs for self-escape from an inner truth with which he feels unable to cope. Goethe's image of the Harper trapped in an ill-lit prison is metaphorical for what Auden later described as being in 'the cell of himself'.[112] In 'An die Türen' he dons a pilgrim's mantle, wandering, with no place at which to arrive, driven by a sense of dislocation, or dissonance. Here his duet with Mignon, 'Nur wer die Sehnsucht kennt', is expressive of a shared sense of displacement and despair, whereby both characters are fractured by guilt, their suffering becoming a sort of expiation, as they seek solace from their own uncomfortable existential condition. The typically modern obsession with the philosophical problem of freedom in relation to responsibility is subtly raised in Goethe's Harper. What we have in the Harper is metaphysical exile – exile from the self in which boundaries of identity are transgressed, yet meaning is disclosed, and the real cause of exile is both revealed and shown to be imaginary.

Seóirse Bodley, 'Nur wer die Sehnsucht kennt'

Apart from Schubert's and Rubenstein's settings, Bodley's setting is one of the few duet settings of this text. Bodley's duet setting of 'Nur wer die Sehnsucht kennt' is entirely faithful to Goethe's novel, where it is described as an irregular duet between Mignon and the Harper, an idea Bodley has used in his setting. Here in Bodley's setting only Mignon sings the complete text, the Harper ruminates softly like an echo of Mignon's thoughts repeating 'ich leide', 'allein', 'es schwindelt mir', 'die Sehnsucht' – ending with a soft 'ich leide' as the music sinks towards silence. Whereas this song is traditionally interpreted as a separation from a lover, the angular nature of Bodley's Adagio lines and disjunct *pianissimo* accompaniment endorse its themes of family severance and exile.

The sparse musical gestures of Bodley's introduction, laden with dramatic tension, (bars 400-404), set the stage for Mignon's proclamation of the duet's central theme: only those who have experienced unfulfilled longing can understand what she suffers. In long expressive lines Mignon stresses how her solitude severs her from all joy as she gazes continually into the heaven's demesne (bars 409-16); the harper's triple *piano* echo, 'ich leide' (bars 408-409), and varied sixfold statement of 'allein' (bars 410-18) is a catatonic version of the lines she sings. This theme of severance is strongly suggested in the wide-

---

112 W.H. Auden, 'In Memory of W.B. Yeats' in *Another Time* (London: Faber & Faber, 1940), p.108, II, 1, p.27.

ranging vocal line and varied dynamics (bars 418-23), with which she ironically endorses her desire for a distant beloved, her ebullition in line ten, 'Es schwindelt mir' (bars 424-25), similarly rendered. As Gretchen in the original version of the spinning song cries: 'Mein Schoos! Gott! drängt / Sich nach ihm hin' (My womb aches for him), in 'Nur wer die Sehnsucht kennt' Mignon breathlessly declaims: 'Es brennt mein Eingeweide' (I am on fire inside, bars 425-26), her reference to viscera playing on the biblical image of the intestines as the seat of emotions.[113] Following this paroxysm of passion, she struggles for self-possession, concluding with a varied statement of the refrain affirming the belief that only one who has known such desire can understand what she endures. Mignon's closing melisma on 'leide' (bars 432-34) is suitably answered by the Harper (bars 436-38) and a sustained dissonant chord voiced *pppp* which closes the cycle.

Seóirse Bodley, *Gretchen* (2012)

Seóirse Bodley's song cycle was specially commissioned for the conference, *Music in Goethe's Faust: Goethe's Faust in Music,* organized at the National University of Ireland, 20-22 April 2012. The premiere took place on 20 April 2012, 8pm and received resounding applause. Gretchen was sensitively sung by Sylvia O'Brien (soprano), the Böser Geist dramatically rendered by Imelda Drumm (mezzo-soprano), the choir members from The Mornington Singers led by Orla Flanagan, and the performance accompanied by Seóirse Bodley (piano).

In the composer's programme note for that evening Bodley reveals:

> From quite early on in composing this cycle I found myself thinking of it as a secular *stations of the cross,* following Gretchen's progress from uneasy awareness of her attraction to Faust to social disapproval, guilt and sorrow.[114]

Bodley's description of Gretchen's story echoes an earlier rendering in his song cycle *A Girl* (1979) in which Brendan Kennelly gives voice to a Kerry girl of sixteen, who drowned herself in response to the social derision her pregnancy evoked. In the programme note he wrote for that performance Bodley described how her songs 'trace her emotions and thoughts as she moves towards the only logical solution that she can see' and are a sympathetic portrayal of someone 'who is pushed to extremes'[115] The poet's recollection of the girl's 'quick, dark way she had of throwing a glance over her shoulder at you as she moved away from you. [...] She always seemed to be moving away into herself'[116] describes a similar trajectory to Gretchen's in these songs.

The narrative of the Gretchen cycle was influenced by the infanticide cases of Goethe's youth. During Goethe's Leipzig years, Catharina Maria Flindt was sentenced to death for killing her illegitimate child. She was rescued from prison by her lover, but beset by guilt, she returned to face her execution. Later, in Frankfurt, in 1772, the 24-year-old Susanna Brandt was publicly executed for infanticide.[117] Goethe was, at this time, working as an

---

[113] Mignon's reference to 'Eingeweide' in line ten is a biblical image drawn from Job 30:27. In Goethe's 'Künstlers Apotheose' the image recurs as 'Die Eingeweide brennen mir', *WA.,* I, 16, p.158.

[114] Seóirse Bodley, Composer's Programme Note, premiere performance, 20 April 2012.

[115] Programme Booklet for the Dublin Festival of Twentieth Century Music (1980), p.12. Cited in Gareth Cox, *Seóirse Bodley* (Dublin: Field Day Press, 2010), p.90.

[116] Ibid, p.91.

[117] The 335-page process document (*Criminalia 1771,* No. 62) is in the Institute for Urban History in Frankfurt. The entire case has been documented in Ruth Berger: *Gretchen. Ein Frankfurter Kriminalfall* (Reinbek: Kindler, 2007); Siegfried Birkner: *Das Leben und Sterben der Kindsmörderin Susanna Margaretha Brandt. Nach den Prozeßakten dargestellt* (Frankfurt: Insel Verlag,1973); Rebekka Habermas (Hrsg.): *Das Frankfurter Gretchen. Der Prozeß gegen die Kindsmörderin Susanna Margaretha Brandt* (Munich: C.H. Beck, 1999); Kent D. Lerch, Jörg Ziethen, Sascha Ziemann, 'Die Leiden des jungen „Gretchen". 'Ein Frankfurter Kriminalfall anno 1771/72: Der Prozess gegen die Kindsmörderin Susanna Margaretha Brandt' in: *Forschung Frankfurt,* Heft 2/2011, pp.49-54.

attorney in Frankfurt and had copies made of the court case documenting the entire process. He was so deeply moved by the tragedy of Susanna Margarete Brandt that it became a central motif in *Urfaust*; a copy of the prison scene still written in prose, the oldest part of the *Urfaust*, dates from shortly after her execution.

While Gretchen's songs from *Faust 1* trace the kernel of that story, they are an analogue of Goethe's preoccupation with the young woman in society (which was naturally in the tradition of *opera comique* and the North German *Singspiel*) where the literary roots of the sentimental woman (*Empfindsame*) or *belle âme* (*schöne Seele*) of *Sturm und Drang* tradition is bound to the psychological stance of a pseudo revolutionary crude bourgeois. If social critique was hardly the sole *raison d'etre* for Gretchen's songs, it nevertheless constitutes a red thread through these settings and makes one realize yet again how deeply implicated in life's labyrinths songs can be.

'Der König in Thule'

'Der König in Thule' was composed by Goethe in 1774 and was recited by the poet to friends in Cologne, on a trip through the Rhineland during that year.[118] The text was first printed in musical form in Seckendorff's *Volks-und andere Lieder*. It was later included in Goethe's *Sammlung* of 1782 and appears in Fräulein von Göchenhausen's manuscript copy of Goethe's *Urfaust*.[119] It was published in *Faust. Ein Fragment* in 1790, revised for Goethe's *Neuen Schriften* in 1800[120] and appeared in the final draft of *Faust 1*.

Gretchen's ballad is composed in six quatrains with the alternative rhyme, *abab*. As with the traditional ballad, the first and third lines are composed in iambic tetrameter, while the second and fourth are scored in iambic trimeter.[121] Although Goethe substitutes dactyls for iambs, rendering a march-like rhythm, this variation does not affect the basic *da capo* form of his poem.[122] Similarly, the number of unaccented syllables varies in each strophe.[123] It is not just the poetic form which mirrors the ballad tradition: its medieval time-frame and mysterious mood is reminiscent of many of the Scots ballads of which Goethe was particularly fond. Like the *Volksballade*, its tale of love is narrated in an objective manner, the action is foreshortened and its diction is simple though its connection with the *Kunstballade* is revealed through its thematic development and use of such compound words as 'Vätersaal', 'Lebensglut' and such archaic forms as 'täten' and 'sinken'.

---

[118] Boyd links the lyric to the *Romanzen und Geistergeschichten* which Goethe read in the Jacobis' home in Frankfurt, *Notes to Goethe's Poems*, vol.1, p.58, a reading which is confirmed in *Dichtung und Wahrheit* III, 15, *HA.*, 10, p.34.

[119] A separate copy of 'Der König in Thule' made by Fräulein von Göchhausen was found in Herder's *Nachlaß*, where it is entitled '*Romanze*'. This manuscript is considered to be Goethe's *Urform*. From Seckendorff's publication, the lyric appears with its existing title.

[120] Goethe's revisions are extensive. The second working is smoother than the original version, in which the poet reproduced the language of the people. It also eliminates the *Sturm und Drang* elements, in the interests of greater literary refinement. In the early rendition, lines two to six read: ' Ein' goldnen Becher er hätt/ Empfangen von seiner Buhle/ Auf ihrem Todesbett. /2. Den Becher hätt er lieber, / Trank draus bei jedem Schmaus'. In stanza three, line ten was written as 'Städt' und 'Reich' in lieu of 'Städt' im Reich' and line eleven included 'seinen Erben' instead of 'seinem Erben'. In verse four, line thirteen, Goethe originally wrote 'Am hohen Königsmahle', whereas lines fifteen and sixteen appeared as 'Im alten Vätersaale/ Auf seinem Schloß am Meer'. Goethe opened the fifth strophe 'Da saß der alte Zecher' and in line nineteen 'heiligen' was written in full. In the final stanza the order of verbs appeared as 'Er sah ihn sinken und trinken/ Und stürzen tief ins Meer', lines twenty-three and twenty-four are separated with a dash, while in the final line 'nie einen Tropfen' originally read as 'keinen Tropfen'.

[121] For an alternative reading see Trunz who reads this metre as spondaic feet, *HA.*, 1, p.495.

[122] Five involve syllables ending in a nasal, which can be read as semi-vocalic; one involves the ending -*e* ('Städt'), often suppressed and one an unstressed *i* between stem and inflectional ending ('heil'gen'), normally suppressed in German iambic verse.

[123] The syllabic count is 8,6,7,7; 7,6,8,6; 7,7,7,6; 6,6,6,6; 7,6,7,6; 7,6,8,6.

'Der König in Thule' is sung by Gretchen during the *Abend* scene.[124] Following her first encounter with Faust on the street, Gretchen returns to her room. The scene opens as she prepares for bed. Momentarily she leaves and during her absence, Faust and Mephistopheles enter her room. Faust is uneasy about being there, his moral sensibility is mocked by Mephistopheles and eventually they leave. On Gretchen's return, she is sensitive to their presence. Frightened by something inexplicable to her, she sings a song to bolster her courage as she undresses for bed.

Although some critics regard the lyric as an *intermezzo*, Gretchen's ballad is significant to this scene. The song of love reveals her preoccupation with the handsome cavalier, whom she desires, as well as fears, to love. Gretchen's love for Faust inspires her with fear, for she senses the prospect of unhappiness in their affair. As she sings of the king's love for a woman probably of lower social rank, this anxiety is unconsciously appeased.[125] Gretchen's lied inspires her with new hope and marks a significant point in the drama: from this scene on, she welcomes his advances.[126] Dramatically, her song is highly effective, for the contrast between this tale and the action on stage heightens the sense of imminent tragedy. Before she sings, Faust's appearance with his daemonic companion presents a sense of impending doom. Through Gretchen's ballad, dramatic irony is reintroduced into the scene, for she cannot know how Faust is to betray her.[127] Gretchen's song suggests how her fate has already begun; she does not know it, nor understand it, yet it is there. Paradoxically, she sings a song of which she knows nothing and yet its theme lies within herself. She tells of a relationship which is not sanctioned by society and the expression of her love, in the form of a mythical folk tale, suggests how its fulfilment can only be imagined.

The location of Goethe's legend is also highly symbolic. In classical antiquity, Thule was an island which marked the northern limits of the known world,[128] and the epithet *ultima* was always applied to it. With its endless days at summer solstice and endless nights at winter solstice, Thule has become a legendary land, which is comparable with the land of the Hyperboreans, so often conjured up by the Greeks in poetry and fable. However, as the Roman philosopher, Seneca, envisaged voyages of discovery to fresh lands beyond these limits, Thule indicates the temporary boundaries of the world. According to the legend, Goethe's citadel is positioned by the sea. What it contains behind its walls is isolated from the rest of the world and so it assumes an aura of remoteness, which makes it as desirable as it is inaccessible. In 'Der König in Thule', Goethe's setting signifies longing for and awareness of the furthest bounds of what is, by

---

[124] *Faust*, 1, ll.2759 to 2782, *HA*, 3, p.89. In the *Urfaust*, the lyric runs from lines 611-34, *HA.*,3, p.390.

[125] The theme of fidelity is uncommon in the German *Volkslied*. It contrasts with Goethe's parodies, 'Heidenröslein' and 'Die Spinnerin', while eight of the twelve ballads which Goethe collected in Alsace share the motif of the unfaithful lover.

[126] Dramatically, the gift of the goblet is also linked to the gift of jewels, which Gretchen discovers after she sings this lied.

[127] Gretchen's song finds a parallel in *Othello* (IV, iii), where Desdemona sings of the tragic love of an ill-fated maid who 'died singing it'. As Desdemona's song of the willow is an emblem of deserted love and portends her death, Gretchen's song signifies her impending fate.

[128] The Ultima Thule of the Romans is known through Vergil and Seneca as an island beyond the northern regions of Britain. Although its precise location is indeterminate, the Greek geographer Pytheas is alleged to have discovered Thule lying six days' sail to the north of Britain and more modern scholars (such as Ptolemäus) identified it with Unst, most northerly of the Shetland Islands. There are various claimants to the title. Some say it was Iceland, others, the Hebrides, still others identify it as Greenland. It was said by ancient geographers to be a six-day ocean journey beyond Britain, a fact which may be symbolized in the six stanzas of this verse. Goethe's interest in the northern regions evolved through his friendship with Herder and in his Straßburg notebook, *Ephemerides,* he records: 'Bücher zur Skaldischen Literatur [...] Olai Wormii litt. Runica [...] Edda. Saxon. Gramm. hist. Danica usw.,' Hermann Hefele, *Geschichte und Gestalt* (Leipzig: Hegner, 1940), p.40; *HA.*, 1, p.495.

its own nature, restricted. In more general terms, the story of a king's fidelity in Ultima Thule subtly signals the limitations of desire.

The image of the *Becher* is also laden with symbolic significance. In Celtic mythology, a goblet filled with wine or mead which a maiden handed to the king elect, was a sign of sovereignty.[129] In 'Der König in Thule' the chalice of kingship is a symbol of the supremacy of love. To exchange cups is a traditional symbol of faithfulness, yet in Goethe's fable, the gift is only given from the girl and this alteration of tradition anticipates the nature of Gretchen's relationship with Faust. The chalice gains religious significance in stanza five as the 'goldnen Becher' is transformed into a 'heiligen Becher'. This supernal quality is supported through the setting, which plays on the association of a cup with profane feasting in the Christian and Jewish tradition,[130] its sacred character being intensified by the fact that it is the King's last supper. Whereas Boyd considers that 'the 'Becher' is holy to the king because of the qualities that are associated with it',[131] its consecrated character is also reminiscent of medieval legends of the holy grail,[132] where the chalice is associated with virginity. As in *Der Becher*, it emerges as a symbol of erotic love,[133] whereby the gift of a goblet is a poetic avowal of the woman's physical surrender.[134] In addition to its amatory associations, Goethe's golden chalice of wine is a traditional vessel of immortality: a symbol of love's eminence and endurance. Whereas in the opening stanza, Goethe plays upon the Bacchic symbolism of wine to denote sexual pleasure and engender intoxication and forgetfulness of all but the beloved,[135] in the final stanza, as the king watches the goblet sink into the sea, its lilting movement suggested through the verbs 'stürzen', 'trinken' and 'sinken' seem to give the chalice automorphic qualities, as it too seems to have the will to die. As it plunges into the sea, the king's eyelids sink[136] and the ensuing silence emulates his final sleep. The sinking goblet symbolizes the end of an age, as his memories of love dissipate into the ocean.

Seóirse Bodley, 'Der König in Thule'

Bodley's ominous introduction immediately announces the contrast between Gretchen's tale and the action on stage. The low octave gesture in the piano prelude at once acknowledges the baleful presence of Mephisto in her room before she sings and his sinister hand in her fate.[137] Gretchen is alive to this unfavourable atmosphere[138] and, as

---

[129] See, for example, the famous legend of *Baile an Scáil*, where the King of Ireland, Conn, watches as a maiden of wondrous beauty hands him the chalice in the presence of the god, Lug, who prophesies that his descendants will reign for many generations.

[130] See for example Psalms 11:6 and 23:5 and Revelation 16:19.

[131] Boyd, I, p.58.

[132] It is interesting to note that the draught of this vessel is blood, the principle of life, and is therefore homogeneous with the heart. Furthermore, its libation, 'Blut', links with the rhyming patterns of lines eighteen and twenty ('Lebensglut' and 'Flut').

[133] In 'Der Becher', written for Charlotte von Stein in September 1781, Goethe gives this image its full sexual significance, *BA.*, 1, pp.346-47, and the metaphor recurs in his letters to her around this time. See for example *Goethe Briefe*, I, Letter no. 298, 31 March 1782, p.386. The motif occurs in Goethe's *Theatralische Sendung*, where Wilhelm expresses his desire for Marianne, as a 'Rausch des Taumelskelches', I, 23; *GA.*, VII, p.578, while in *Tasso* the image of a brimming goblet is symbolic of intense love, *Tasso*, V, 4. ll. 3267-68, *HA.*, 3, p.161.

[134] The representation of the cup as the human body reappears in the final stanza, where it is personified in lines 2779 and 2780, *HA, 3*, p.89.

[135] This motif also recurs in the opening stanza of 'Der Becher', where Goethe writes: 'Einen wohlgeschnitten vollen Becher / Hielt ich drückend in den beiden Händen, / Sog begierig süßen Wein vom Rande, / Gram und Sorg auf einmal zu vertrinken' (Pressed between both hands I held a full, beautifully fashioned cup, and greedily sucked sweet wine from its rim, to drink away all my sorrow and care), *BA.*, p.346.

[136] In line twenty-three Goethe writes 'Die Augen täten ihm sinken': *täten* is not a subjunctive but an old form of the past indicative. As in English, the verb, 'do' used to be common as an auxilary in colloquial German ('his eyes, they did drop').

[137] *Faust*, Abend, ll.2684-2752.

Bodley's performance indication in bar 6 implies, she sings this ballad in an absentminded manner to appease her fears. With the exception of stanzas one and two, which are run together as in Schubert's setting, allusions to this musical gesture recur in between strophes so that the listener is continually imbued with a sense of imminent tragedy. A good example of this is found in the recapitulation of the opening pianistic gesture between stanzas two and three, where the time frame of the ballad changes and the poet portrays the king in his final hours.

The irregularity with which this figure reappears is mirrored in Bodley's largely through-composed melody, which bears something of the character of a folksong, although it is too wide-ranging to belong to this tradition. Bodley's coupling of the first two stanzas in one strophe pays homage to the balladic tradition, while his allusion to the ballad form is also evident in the fourth and fifth strophes, which hinge around each other, jointly portraying the king's last supper, its lofty, remote location in the hall of his forefathers underscored by *sostenuto* chords (bars 45-46) – the only *forte* dynamic in this song. Bodley's mirroring of musical material in stanzas four and five salutes this strophic structure, and its transposition a tone higher (from bar 50f.) locates this serpentine repetition in an asymmetrical setting.

One other musical gesture is central to this song. The symbolic nature of the gift of a golden goblet, which the king's concubine grants him on her death-bed,[139] is underscored by cascading, descending thirds (bars 6-7), later shared by voice and piano to convey the King's overflowing tears (bars 22-25).[140] These parallel thirds which underscore the King's lifelong fidelity recur at the end of his life (bars 30-38), where he numbers the cities of his kingdom and bequeaths everything to his heirs, except his goblet of gold. It, like the memory of his love, belongs to him alone. The descending lines of bars 51-58 in piano and voice, and cascading thirds which once illustrated the flow of tears, now encapsulate the king's imbibing of the 'letzte Lebensglut' before he hurls the 'heiligen Becher' (bar 54) into the sea.[141] Its subsequent descent is accompanied by cascading thirds, its lilting movement suggested by the verbs 'stürzen', 'trinken', musically realized in Bodley's rocking triplet figuration. The psychological realism of Bodley's recurring bass motif (bars 70-76) heralds Gretchen's return to reality and reminds us that Goethe's king is an ideal to be realized. Being positioned in Thule, he ceases to hold any historic significance and becomes a personification of an ethical or psychological quality, an archetype of human perfection and fidelity.

'Gretchen am Spinnrade'

The date of 'Gretchen am Spinnrade' is uncertain. Some critics place it in 1774, others at the end of 1775. There are three versions of the monologue. The earliest manuscript is found in Fräulein von Göchhausen's copy of the *Urfaust*[142] or *Faust in ursprünglicher Gestalt*. The lyric also appears in Herder's copy of the text and in *Faust. Ein Fragment* composed in 1790.[143]

---

[138] Ibid., ll.2753-2864.

[139] Almost fifty years later Goethe intertwined joy and sorrow in this image as a symbol of his love for Ulrike von Levetzow, writing: 'So begreifst du das Bittersüsse des Kelchs, den ich bis auf die Neige getrunken und ausgeschlürft habe' (*JA.*, 18, VIII, 1823).

[140] The expression 'gingen über' which Goethe uses for the King's overflowing tears is drawn from the Lutheran bible, where 'Und Jesu gingen die Augen über' is written in John 11: 23, HA.,1, p.495. Similarly in Clavigo, Act II, 'Das Haus des Clavigo', Goethe writes 'Mein Herz geht mir über', HA., 4, p.275.

[141] The deletion in line 2776: 'Trank letzte Lebensglut' is continued in the closing line of stanza six: 'Trank nie ein Tropfen mehr', both of which are examples of the use of 'popular language' in the *Volksballade*.

[142] ll.1066-1105, *HA*, 3, pp.404-05.

[143] The variations between these copies are minor. In Fräulein von Göchhausen's manuscript 'Lächlen' is used on line twenty-three, whereas in Herder's copy it is altered to 'Lächeln'. In both

Goethe's lyric constitutes an entire scene in Goethe's *Faust*.[144] The episode is entitled *Gretchens Stube* (Gretchen's Room) and the stage direction reads: 'Gretchen am Spinnrade allein'. In Goethe's *Urfaust* and in *Faust. Ein Fragment, Gretchens Stube* was originally placed between *Ein Gartenhäusgen* and *Marthens Garten*, whereas in *Faust. Erster Teil*, Goethe positions it after the *Wald und Höhle* scene; the varied position of this scene also endorses how Gretchen's words do not unveil her circumstances but her state of mind. When Gretchen meets Faust in the *Garten* scene, she discloses her awareness of the social difference between them. She professes an innocence, confirmed through the game she plays in plucking the petals of a daisy to ascertain whether Faust loves her – a gesture of innocence which leads Faust to confess his love for her.[145] Whereas in the *Ein Gartenhäuschen* scene he kisses her, signalling a new level of intimacy, in the following *Wald und Höhle* scene, he recognizes their incompatibility and withdraws from her to the forest. Mephisto seeks him out and tempts him to return by painting a calamitous picture of Gretchen's plight:

Die Zeit wird ihr erbärmlich lang;	To her the time is miserably long
Sie steht am Fenster, sieht die Wolken ziehn	She haunts her window, watching clouds stray
Über die alte Stadtmauer hin.	Over the old city wall and far away.
Wenn ich ein Vöglein wär! so geht ihr Gesang	'Were I a little bird', so runs her song
Tage lang, halbe Nächte lang.	Through half the night and all day long.
Einmal ist sie munter, meist betrübt;	Sometimes she is cheerful, mostly sad;
Einmal recht ausgeweint,	Sometimes she has spent all her tears,
Dann wieder ruhig, wie's scheint,	Then she is tranquil again, so it appears
Und immer verliebt[146]	And always in love

– a predicament which is here confirmed in *Gretchens Stube*. Through the inclusion of the *Wald und Höhle* scene in *Faust. Part I*, Goethe not only endorses Gretchen's frame of mind, but confirms that she is not alone in her suffering. Goethe's incorporation of this scene into *Faust* makes it apparent that Faust's union with Gretchen is not one of nihilistic indifference, yet, by composing this episode as a dramatic monologue, the poet intensifies Gretchen's isolation.

Gretchen's lyric consists of ten short stanzas. Each verse is composed as a quatrain and the first strophe repeated for verses four and eight. The poem is written in the form of a *Volkslied*, where the repetition of the opening strophe replaces a traditional refrain. This two-fold repetition divides this tableau into three distinct episodes: episode one (verses one to three) reveals Gretchen's despair; episode two (stanzas four to seven) conveys her obsession with Faust, and in episode three (verses eight to ten) she expresses an intense desire for Faust. The lyrical nature of each of these episodes is supported through the form and rhythms of the verse. In *Gretchens Stube* the lines are metered in iambic dimeter, though, with the exception of verses three and ten, this metre is modified slightly in each strophe.[147] The rhythms accord with the movement of the spinning wheel and capture the dramatic intensity of the mantra which continually runs in her mind. Whereas the short rhymed lines retain the simplicity of a *Volkslied*, the staccato

---

of these editions, line thirty-five is composed as 'Mein Schoos! Gott! drängt', which was later changed to 'Mein Busen drängt'. In Herder's document line thirty-five is printed as 'dörft' in lieu of 'dürft'.

[144] 'Gretchens Stube', *Faust 1*, Lines 3374 to 3413, *HA*, 3, pp.107-09.

[145] Ironically, after she plucks the last petal, Faust tells Gretchen, 'O schaudere nicht', l. 3188, *HA*, 3, p.102. Both recognize in this shudder the doom allegorically executed upon the flower that bears her name.

[146] ll.3315-23, *HA*, 3, p.106.

[147] See, for example, lines one and five which open with anapaestic feet.

monologue subtly captures the impetuosity of her thoughts and creates a mounting climax in episodes two and three. The musicality of her verse, maintained through the rhyming scheme, also endorses the dramatic development of her lines. Stanzas one, three, (four), six to ten are linked through an *abcb* figure, the second verse is composed in rhyming couplets, *aabb*, while stanza five is written in alternative rhyme, *abab*. The repetition of the refrain is intensified by the urgent rhythm of the poem, heightened by the poetic enjambment between stanzas six and seven (episode two), nine and ten (episode three).

The accompaniment of the spinning wheel in *Gretchens Stube* underscores the themes of Gretchen's song. The spinning wheel is a symbol of the domestic arts, signifying the difference between Gretchen and Faust. As an act of creating, it is a traditional symbol of fertility, which once again augurs her fate: as spinning is equivalent to bringing forth and fostering life. In *Faust* the role of the spinning wheel is fascinating. Whereas Gretchen's lied expresses an outer passivity in relation to her love for Faust, traditionally the spinster is portrayed as a woman of power. Through this motif, Goethe implies how his heroine's role is not entirely passive to her fate. As in folk mythology, where spinners perpetually open and close the cycles which affect individuals and the cosmos, Gretchen is mistress of her own fate. The poet observes the traditional role of the spinner by endowing her with a harsh lineament of fate; as Gretchen spins, the regular turning of the spindle propounds the inevitability of this fate.[148] The repetitive motion of the wheel symbolizes an unyielding circle of inescapable desire. Conversely, as a symbol of renewal, its ceaseless turning portends a new cycle in her relationship with Faust: the dawn of desire and sexual initiation.[149] In conclusion, though *Gretchens Stube* is composed as a lyrical monologue, the poem is not merely lyrical nor subjective, but signifies an ideological and dramatically human turning point and is symbolic of Gretchen's developing character.

Seóirse Bodley, 'Gretchen am Spinnrade'

The appropriation of the song's title from the stage direction 'Gretchen am Spinnrade allein' and opening musical gesture signal Bodley's homage to Schubert. In contrast to the dual perspective of Schubert's famous six-note piano figuration which emulates the spinning wheel and the protagonist's inner turmoil, Bodley's more swiftly-moving four-note figuration only loosely suggests a spinning motif and represents much more the internal workings of Gretchen's mind. Unlike Schubert's richly-allusive accompanying motif, Bodley's laden musical gesture is discontinuous to indicate how her mind is darting from one thing to another: it is broken at the beginnings of the first and third statements of Gretchen's refrain in which she foresees that she will never regain her former tranquillity.[150] Most significantly it is replaced for ten of the twelve lines of episodes two and three and only returns for the two poetic and musical climaxes, where once again, Schubert's musical presence is acknowledged.

The second significant musical gesture of this song is the parallel contrary motion fifths motif in bars 92-93 which heralds a change of modality at the beginning of episode one (stanzas two and three) and highlights how Gretchen's song marks a turning point in

---

[148] This motif is introduced in *Vorspiel auf dem Theater*, l.142, *HA*, 3, p.13; the spinning motif recurs in *Nacht*, ll.503-06, *HA*, 3, p.24, and in *Abend*, ll.2715-16, *HA*, p. 87.

[149] Michael Neumann reads the concept of the Eternal-Feminine in terms of erotic love in *'Die Dialektik der Liebe'* in *Das Ewig-Weibliche in Goethes Faust* (Heidelberg: Carl Winter, 1985), pp.285-306. Contrarily, Barbara Becker Cantarino links Gretchen's sexuality to the demonic in 'Witch and Infanticide: Imaging the Female in *Faust 1*, *Goethe Yearbook* 7 (1994), pp.1-22; here p.8.

[150] In line three 'nimmer' is archaic for 'nie', from 'nie mehr' – which would render 'nimmermehr' tautologous, were it not for the fact that the etymological identity of 'nimmer' and 'nie mehr' is not remembered.

her relationship with Faust.[151] In this scene she is no longer the ingenuous child[152] over whom Mephistopheles claimed to have no power;[153] her sexuality has been awakened by Faust and without him her whole world turns bitter. Bodley's replacement of the original accompaniment figuration underscores this transformation and his interplay of three motifs – parallel fifths (bars 92-93 and 96), a tertial motif (bar 92) developed in bars 97-98 each answered by the 'spinning motif' (bars 94-95) – underscores Gretchen's dependence on Faust, who ominously claims every place is her grave when he is not there.[154] The image of the tomb portrays the abyss in which she is engulfed (paradoxically accompanied by a loss of tranquillity) [155] and portends a blind surrender to the unknown. Bodley draws attention to this ineluctable darkness with a resumption of the 'spinning' motif (bar 99) and a varied restatement of her opening refrain (bars 106-111).

Bodley's treatment of Goethe's two poetic climaxes is also highly significant. In the second episode Gretchen confirms Mephistopheles's picture of her as she tells us how she watches at the window for Faust, who has become her only reason for living. Gretchen's remembrance of Faust is again underscored by the parallel fifths gesture which is augmented to a more stately minim movement in contrary motion parallel 6ths for a description of his features: his nobility of mien, his smile and his eyes. As Gretchen completes this portrait in a succession of ever-more insistent erotic memories in stanza seven, the first poetic and musical climax is reached. Once again the homage to Schubert is announced in the musical gesture B flat to C flat (bars 136-37), the memory of which interrupts the 'spinning' motif in a sustained A flat minor chord over a dissonant left hand chord in which a low A flat and G flat are voiced together. As in Schubert's setting, the 'spinning' motif is hesitantly resumed (bars 138-40). In contrast to Schubert's setting the sudden chromatic shift from A flat to A (bar 143) in Bodley's lead-over passage in D flat major (bars 141-43) displaces us in a different tonality for Gretchen's opening cry, 'Meine Ruh ist hin/ Mein Herz ist schwer' now voiced over hovering semiquavers, F and G (bars 144-48), attended by a very solid statement of the protagonist's loss of peace (bars 149-52).

In the third and final episode Gretchen longs for Faust[156] and acknowledges the abyss which darkens their affair. Her mental agitation, reflected in the disordered syntax of stanza ten, is musically underscored by the transformation of one of the paired parallel fifths into fourths (bars 153-56). Gretchen's desire to kiss Faust is deliberately accentuated by the parallel fifths motif in minim chords (bars 157-58). So too the return of the *fortissimo* two-note semiquaver motif at the second summit of the poem (bars 159-60) underscores her avowal that she would die on his kisses, the voice confiscating the semiquaver runs (bar 161), repossessed by the piano in a triple *forte* climax (bars 162-65). Although this Liebestod imagery is often read as a euphemism for a sexual climax, Gretchen's sequestration of the 'spinning' motif also foregrounds her impending fate. To die is to embrace the unknown: unlike in stanza two, she is no longer afraid, but acknowledges it as an inescapable destiny.

---

[151] In collating the two lyrics, it is interesting to compare Gretchen's reference to the grave with that in 'Der König in Thule', where love is true 'bis an das Grab'. In 'Gretchen am Spinnrade', the image of the tomb carries more sinister implications, auguring her imminent doom.
[152] l.3007, *HA*, 3, p.96.
[153] l.2626, *HA*, 3, p.84.
[154]'Wo' can be read as spatial 'where' or temporal 'when' and probably both senses are contained here.
[155] 'Verrückt' does not specifically mean the adjective 'crazy', although the latter is derived from this word, but rather the past participle 'verrückt' – from 'ver' ('mis') plus 'rücken' (move), meaning 'displace, disarrange, derange, disturb, confuse'.
[156] In Goethe's *Urfaust*, these lines originally read 'Mein Schoos! Gott! drängt/ Sich nach ihm hin'.

'Gretchen im Zwinger'

As the title suggests, 'Gretchen im Zwinger' is from the *Zwinger* scene from Goethe's *Faust, Teil I*.[157] The scene is included in Goethe's *Urfaust*[158] and in this edition, as in *Part One*, it comes after *Am Brunnen*, where Gretchen meets Lieschen at the well. Lieschen informs Gretchen about Bärbelchen's pregnancy and when Gretchen expresses compassion for Bärbelchen's plight, Lieschen condemns her. She continues to tell Gretchen how Bärbelchen's lover has left her, for he would not be such a fool as to marry her. On the way home, Gretchen admits how she too would once have reproached Bärbelchen's actions and the scene concludes as she recognizes herself in the same situation and yet considers:

> Doch alles, was dazu mich trieb,   Yet all that drove me to it –
> Gott! war so gut! ach war so lieb![159]   God! – was so good, so dear.

Recognizing her ostracism from society, Gretchen turns to religion in the following scene. The stage directions at the beginning of this scene *Zwinger* (Inside the town wall) reads: 'In der Mauerhöhle ein Andachtsbild der Mater dolorosa, Blumenkrüge davor' (in the niche of a wall a shrine, with an image of the Mater dolorosa. Pots of flowers before it). Symbolically, the shrine is on the outskirts of the town, which indicates how Gretchen is cast outside the pale of society. Gretchen appears here alone, and as she fills the pots with fresh flowers she speaks to us of her grief.

Gretchen's prayer is arranged in eight sections. The first three parts are written in tercets, with the rhyming scheme, *aab ccb ddb*. Although this strophic opening reflects the form of a prayer, Goethe alters the rhythm in stanzas four and five, which are composed as sestets, sharing a similar end-rhyme: *eefeef gghggh*. The following three strophes are composed as quatrains. In verse six, the second and fourth lines rhyme (*ijkj*); stanza seven is created with alternative rhyme (*lmlm*), while the final strophe recalls the rhymes of the opening stanza, now arranged as *abba*. The scene is composed in madrigal verse and its lines are freely metered in bacchic and iambic feet. This is the first time that Gretchen's lines are couched in this rhythm and the poetic variation again signals her change of fate. In contrast with the realistic dialogue of the previous scene, the monodramatic lyricism of *Zwinger* highlights Gretchen's isolation. Despite this expressively irregular metre, Gretchen's lines are rhymed as in traditional madrigal verse. The rhyme-scheme is strict and strongly reminiscent of the medieval sequence, the *Stabat mater*,[160] and the forms of seventeenth-century German hymnody, to which explicit allusion is made.

Gretchen's supplication to the Virgin Mary in *Zwinger* is emblematic of her suffering, and a poignant play on the old antithesis of Mary and Eve (Ave-Eva) takes on a new form in a secular world. The transformation of desire into penitence appears to constitute what is traditionally attributed to the Virgin, yet Goethe does not present the neo-classical personification of Mary as Virgin mother in this scene, but the *Mater Dolorosa*, the suffering mother of God. Gretchen's prayer to a mother, who is both virginal and

---

[157] ll.3587-3619, *HA*, 3, pp.114-15.

[158] ll.1278-1310, *HA*, 3, pp. 411-12. The alterations are minor. Line three reads 'Dein Antlitz ab zu meiner Not'; the second and third tercets are arranged as a sestet, 'Mit tausend Schmerzen' in line five, while the exclusion of the 'e' in seine is unmarked. Similarly in line twenty-three, the verb ending is not inscribed and ach is followed with an exclamation mark, rather than a comma. However, in line thirty, the exclamation mark after 'Hilf' is excluded, as the meaning is changed from 'Hilf rette mich' to 'Hilf! rette mich' in *Faust I*.

[159] *Faust I, Am Brunnen*, *HA*., 3, ll. 3585-86, p.114.

[160] The sequence is sometimes referred to as *Stabat mater dolorosa* (sorrowfully his mother stood).

maternal, underscores her own loss of innocence.[161] As a religious symbol of motherhood, the *Mater Dolorosa* functions as a substitute for Gretchen's mother, thereby reinforcing her isolation. Alternatively, the shrine of the *Mater Dolorosa* can be read as a transfigured image of Gretchen's suffering and augurs her fate. It introduces a sublime symbol of a mother's sorrow at the loss of her child, a suffering which Gretchen must later experience. The statue before which she kneels depicts Mary's anguish as she witnesses her son 'despised and rejected of men'. Gretchen draws inspiration from this image, where solitude and rejection are acknowledged and transcended through faith. The image of the *Mater Dolorosa* is a visual epitome of Gretchen's affliction. Whether this affliction is the discovery of pregnancy, the death of her mother or fear of abandonment by Faust is unclear. While Gretchen prays to be spared the coming torments of social disgrace and death, she pours her suffering into the traditional forms of worship, which her life has always held for her, and in turning to religion, longs for forgiveness. That she turns to the *Mater Dolorosa* is deeply symbolic. As within the Christian iconographical tradition, the *Mater Dolorosa* personifies courage and is an incarnation of Eternal Forgiving Love.

Seóirse Bodley, 'Gretchen im Zwinger'

Bodley's opening gesture honours the Stabat Mater tradition in the simple F major, g minor and a minor chords (bars 166, 168-69) whose spread is so wide-ranging, so separated in sonority that they can no longer be placed within their classical context. This gesture recurs in stanza five (bars 195-201) where Gretchen's sorrow is underpinned by similar reconfigurations of classical chords which render a very different sonority. A further example is found in the descending high chords of the penultimate strophe (bars 212-12), displaced by a dissonant bass underpinning Gretchen's mounting anguish.

In the opening refrain Gretchen addresses the *Mater Dolorosa*, Our Lady of Sorrows, in long lyrical lines of supplication, imploring her to look upon her in her hour of affliction. She develops this religion of the Cross in the descending lines of the second strophe in which she sees the mother of God, looking upon her son, her heart pierced with a sword.[162] The empathy she feels with the *Mater Dolorosa* is subtly symbolized in Bodley's doubling of the vocal line; the thousand-fold grief she suffers, answered by the onset of an increasing chromaticism (bars 178-79), is developed in the third strophe, where Gretchen imagines Mary asking God, the Father, to have mercy on her son's affliction. The gradual chromatic descent from A to D sharp (bars 180-82) calls attention to this traditional role of Mary as mediator, to whom Gretchen turns for divine intercession.

The suffering of the Divine Mother is also acknowledged in a rising gesture C-D-E flat and its restatement as an inverted cluster (bars 184-85). Gretchen's identification with the *Mater Dolorosa* is subtly acknowledged by this shared musical gesture (F-E-D, bars 188-90; A-G-F sharp, bar 191 and E-F sharp-G, bars 193-94). In Bodley's rendering, Gretchen's music appropriates the musical symbolism of the *Stabat Mater* because hers is a supreme sorrow, no less terrible than that of a mother who watches her child die. This association is continued in the falling thirds in the piano, left hand (bars 192-94), which link the fourth and fifth strophes, where the tertiary motif recurs in her vocal line (bars 187-193 and 195-204) and introduces stanza seven (bars 2010-11), in which the minor third gesture reappears (bars 216-18 and 220-21). The scene closes with a recapitulation of Gretchen's petition to the *Mater Dolorosa* (bars 223-26), now closing

---

[161] As a surrogate mother to her little sister, now deceased, Gretchen has already experienced this state.

[162] This image stems from Luke, 2, 35; it is traditionally used in the *Stabat mater dolorosa*, in the sequence, *Planctus ante nescia* and is a common motif in medieval lyrics which portray Mary's sorrow.

on a *pianissimo* F major chord (bar 226). The piano echoes her supplication with a recapitulation of the prelude before closing on an F major chord.

'Szene aus Goethes *Faust*'

Goethe's *Dom* (Cathedral) scene from *Faust, Teil I* develops and intensifies the themes of the *Zwinger* scene.[163] In the previous scene, Faust wounds Gretchen's brother, Valentin, in a duel. Gretchen enters to discover her brother dying and yet his final moments are spent reproaching her for her loss of innocence. He paints a bleak picture of her future and tells her it is her ignominy which has pierced his heart. Isolated by his lack of compassion, Gretchen seeks solace in religion. She enters the cathedral in search of forgiveness, but is immediately overpowered by guilt, externalized in the form of the evil spirit. She finds the cathedral spiritually and physically asphyxiating, yet she does not turn her back on her faith. Standing amid the devout congregation of worshippers, Gretchen feels the sting of her sinful isolation even more sharply than if she were alone. As a silent and forbidding presence – a ghostly reminder of her former self – the congregation intensifies the bitterness of her moral seclusion.

In the cathedral scene, Goethe composes Gretchen's and the *Böser Geist's* lines in free verse. Their speeches are unmetered, unrhymed and irregularly lined. The balanced phrasing and syntactical repetition in their lines lends a sense of immediacy to the episode, which could not be so vividly conveyed in regularly metered, rhymed and structured verse. The pacing and cadence of their thoughts is varied according to syntactical, breath and conversational units, which frame the lineation and rhythm of the poem. The extensive variation in rhythm supports the alternation of their voices in the scene. In contrast to this use of free verse, Goethe composes the choral entries in strict time. The verses of the *Dies Irae* are composed in trochaic tetrameter. Each of the choral entries is created with a single rhyme: the first, a rhyming couplet: *aa* (lines twenty-three to twenty-four); followed by two rhymed tercets, *bbb* and *ccc* (lines thirty-seven to thirty-nine; forty-nine to fifty-one); concluding with a single entry, *d* (line fifty-seven).

Gretchen's feelings of isolation from humanity deflect the drama onto a psychological plane. Although spoken, her lines represent an externalization of her inner thoughts and may be read as a soliloquy or interior monologue. Gretchen's prayer is marked by frequent interruptions. Using a dramatic technique that dates back to the mediaeval morality plays, Goethe turns the scene into a quasi-dialogue by embodying the pestering inner voice of Gretchen's conscience into an actual character – a vexatious evil spirit who whispers in her ear. Gretchen hears its vicious insinuations as a voice from within, but the audience sees it as an actual character. As the *Böser Geist* represents an inner voice, the choir present an external one. Gretchen apprehends their solemn chanting as a dire warning directed towards herself. Reverberating through the cathedral with the support from the deep, sombre tones of the organ, this ominous musical voice interrupts Gretchen's monologue in three different places, as if forcing its message upon her. Whereas the Evil Spirit addresses Gretchen directly, the chorus serves as an equally effective dramatic vehicle for augmenting her sense of guilt. As each competes for Gretchen's attention, the dramatic tension steadily mounts, culminating in her collapse at the end of the scene.

Goethe's autonomous presentation of Gretchen's Evil Spirit is not unique to the cathedral scene. Greek mythology is replete with accounts of struggles with grotesque beings[164] which represent earlier stages of human consciousness or untransformed forces at work in man's soul. In *Klassische Walpurgisnacht*[165] Goethe presents a vast 'landscape of the soul' in which mythological beasts reflect qualities residing in the depths of man's

---

[163] ll.3776-3834, *HA*, 3, pp.120-21.
[164] For example, Perseus and Medusa, Odysseus and the Cyclops.
[165] *Faust II*, *HA*., 3, p.215.

consciousness. As the Fool in Shakespeare's *King Lear* represents the Voice of Consciousness, Goethe presents this concept in a negative guise through the figure of the *Böser Geist*. In the Cathedral scene, the Evil Spirit emerges as a lurid being, who, like Mephisto, is portrayed as a dramatic character. Through this separate portrayal, Goethe depicts evil as a very real force and conveys how Gretchen experiences evil as a reality. In the cathedral scene the *Böser Geist* is not just a mere component of her 'subjectivity', but a motive force within her person. He personifies the cosmic force of opposition and his derision delineates the assault of the 'Anti I' upon the 'I'. The Evil Spirit is the synthesis of all those powers which lead to the disintegration of the personality. As a symbol of evil, he depicts the forces which disturb, cloud and weaken Gretchen's consciousness, driving it to indeterminacy and ambivalence. The scene presents Gretchen's struggle against the diabolical possibilities within herself; her struggle for the preservation of good above this force.[166]

Gretchen's *Böser Geist* constitutes an aspect of her own psychological-historical development. By dividing her inner conflict between two individual characters, Goethe illustrates Gretchen's pre-individual consciousness, which still experiences evil as a spiritual force outside the self. The Evil Spirit represents an archaic mode of consciousness, of which she is part. As Gretchen enters the cathedral her old form of consciousness rises to the surface and provides outdated 'ideals'. She thinks, feels and acts in harmony with the age-old traditions which attach to groups in which she is at home and does not question the values they uphold. Though she is ostracized by society, her morality is still part of a group consciousness. She enters the church believing her innocence, yet the Evil Spirit's derision deprives her of her deep-felt purity.[167] Through his ceaseless contention, Gretchen contends with the censure which she has internalized.[168]

Seóirse Bodley, 'Szene aus Goethes Faust'

Bodley deliberately sets the Böser Geist in a contrasting mezzo-soprano voice to signal the character as an *externalization* of Gretchen's inner thoughts. Following a two-bar opening gesture the *Böser Geist* immediately taunts Gretchen with memories of her former innocence. Her derision is voiced in major and minor ninths (bars 254-58) where she inquires what deeds of shame lurk in her heart. The accompanying tremolandi (bars 259-62), recurrence of the opening gesture (bars 264, 265 and 267) and development of the descending scale motif (bars 270-71) which accompanied her glissando on 'Gretchen' (bar 253) underscore the Evil Spirit's insinuations that Gretchen has induced her mother's death.[169] Her final intimation, where she alludes to the presence of Gretchen's unborn child, is again characterised by major and minor 7ths (bars 272 and 274) and underscored by the opening gesture in the accompaniment (bar 276).

With the *Böser Geist*'s third accusation, the tremolandi which initially foregrounded the allusion to her mother's death recur (bars 280-82) as Gretchen calls out for relief from the pain of remorse. Her cry of remission that she cannot arrest her thoughts (bar 283-88) confirms that the *Böser Geist* is the voice of her own conscience which combines the voices of self-reproach, public blame and divine condemnation, offering no relief

---

[166] Gretchen's inner turmoil, like that of the Harper, can also be interpreted as the destruction by guilt. For Goethe, as for Schiller, 'der Übel größtes aber ist die Schuld' (Schiller, *Die Braut von Messina, Schillers Werke* (Switzerland: Verlag Birkhäuser-Basel, 1943), p.413.

[167] Whereas in *Am Brunnen* Gretchen had refused to submit or to allow to be tarnished that which she, in her unsophisticated and confused confession, had justified before God, 'Und bin ich nun selbst der Sünde bloß! / Doch – alles, was dazu mich trieb / Gott! war so gut! ach war so lieb', ll.113-14, *HA*, 3, p.114, in the cathedral she succumbs.

[168] This trait is also evident in the final *Kerker* scene, where she assigns the mother the role of a whore, l.4412, *HA*, 3, p.139.

[169] This is the first time the death of Gretchen's mother is mentioned and so the news renders the highest intensity in this scene.

from any side. Gretchen's inability to relinquish this inner reprehension before which she now stands condemned is voiced in an insistent melody of repeated notes (bars 283, 285 and 287).

A *fortissimo* staccato g minor chord, reconfigured from the classical tradition (bar 289), heralds the first choral entry (bar 290), where the choir intones the first section of the Requiem Mass in a very threatening manner as Gretchen perceives it. Ostensibly, the verses bear no direct relation to her: she has entered the cathedral during a Requiem Mass, the occasion for which has nothing to do with her sorrowful predicament.[170] Yet the sections the choir intone from the liturgy of the dead heighten Gretchen's plight. The *fortissimo* lines of the *Dies Irae* which relate the horrors of Judgement Day (bars 290-93) beat remorselessly on her ears, its message as merciless as the spirit's words. The g minor modality of this choral passage is taken up by the Evil Spirit who extends this theme in the following strophe, where she paints a traditional picture of trombones sounding and bodies rising from the graves, her admonition underscored by *fortissimo* descending staccato octaves (bars 296-99). The Evil Spirit's placing of Gretchen in this setting, seized with horror, in fear of God's final edict, is underpinned by a descending tertiary motif (bars 300-304) and cascading thirds which fall to a low F (bars 305-06). In contrast to the solace Gretchen sought in entering the cathedral, her desire to be elsewhere is underscored by heavy chords, her admission of how stifled she feels by the choral intonations is pointed by her appropriation of the Evil Spirit's 7th motif (bar 313). Her awareness of the music signals the second choral entry, where the choral recitation of verse six of the Requiem Mass is effectively doubled an octave higher in the accompaniment (bars 318-20). Although 24 bars of dialogue have passed 'between' Gretchen and the *Böser Geist*, the omission of four verses from the *Dies Irae* conveys the passage of time and the nightmare quality of Goethe's scene, where Gretchen's psychological turmoil moves at a different pace to 'reality'. In bars 318-23 the choir relates how, on the final day, God will sit in judgement; anything which lies hidden will then appear and nothing shall remain unavenged. Observing their words, Gretchen's third monologue, heralded by a crotchet triplet motif (bar 324), becomes increasingly hysterical. Her description of how the church atmosphere suffocates her, the pillars of the wall imprison her, the vaulted roof weighs down upon her are again characterized by the minor 7th leaps (bars 327-28 and 329-30) which the Böser Geist first sang when alluding to Gretchen's misdeeds (bars 257-58). As Gretchen cries out for air, the descending octave on 'Luft' conveys her feeling of breathlessness.

Instead of the relief she seeks, the Evil Spirit returns, reconfiguring Gretchen's triplet motif in diminution (bars 338-39) as she whispers to Gretchen that even if she hid, her sin and shame would not be concealed. In their third entry (bars 344-49), the choir adopt Gretchen's position, as they ask, 'What then shall a wretched one as I say?' Their subsequent question, 'What protector shall I ask, when scarcely a just man may be free from care?' is particularly poignant, for though Gretchen has entered the church in search of relief, she has found no comfort.

In a final insidious speech, the *Böser Geist* informs Gretchen how the glorified turn their faces from her and the pure shudder to reach to her (bars 350-60). The final choral entry repeats the questions 'Quid sum miser tunc dicturus?/Quem patronum rogaturus' in a threatening whisper (bars 362-65),[171] interrupted by Gretchen's cry for help. She faints before the *Dies Irae* makes its turn at the verse 'Recordare Jesu pie', where the theme of Divine judgement is replaced by an annunciation of the compassion of Christ. The whirring scale passages in octaves which strike up in the piano (bars 366-372) impel

---

[170] Originally, Goethe intended the Requiem for Gretchen's mother; by altering this intent, Goethe transforms her suffering from public to private sorrow and heightens the solitary nature of her suffering.

[171] This reiteration is not included in the text of the Mass; Bodley here extends Goethe's repetition to two lines.

the scene to a dramatic close. Gretchen's continual self-torment makes it impossible for her to go on; her collapse at the end of the scene, symbolized in the final musical gesture, a *sforzando* E, is paradigmatic of her physical and psychological demise.

'Meine Mutter, die Hur'

1. Prehistory and Origins of the Scene: Gretchen's final song of madness dates from 1773 and one of the earliest Faust scenes. There are three versions of the monologue. The earliest manuscript is found in Fräulein von Göchhausen's copy of the *Urfaust*[172] or *Faust in ursprünglicher Gestalt*. The lyric also appears in Herder's copy of the text. While it was the last of the final three scenes – *Nacht, Nacht. Offen Feld*, and *Kerker* – omitted from *Faust. Ein Fragment* (1790), Goethe reinserted it in *Faust 1*.

Gretchen's song of madness is composed in nine lines of free verse with an irregular rhyming scheme:

Meine Mutter, die Hur	My mother, the whore!
Die mich umgebracht hat!	Who killed me dead
Mein Vater, der Schelm	My father, the rogue
Der mich gessen hat!	Who ate my flesh?
	!
Mein Schwesterlein klein	Little sister gathered
Hub auf die Bein,	The bones he scattered;
An einem kühlen Ort;	In a cool, cool place they lie
Da ward ich ein schönes Waldvöglein,	And there I became a tiny bird so fine,
Fliege fort, fliege fort!	Fly away, fly away!

The lines are irregularly lined out: the opening line opens with an anapaest followed by an iambic beat; line three a bachic foot followed by an iambic beat; line 5 an iambic foot followed by an iambic beat whereas line 9 is made up of two anapaests. These changing metres are alternated with freely-metered lines of varied syllabic lengths. The balanced phrasing of the first three couplets – 'Meine Mutter...'; 'Mein Vater...'; 'Mein Schwesterlein klein' – are structured on semiformal speech rhythms which depend on a sense of pacing and rhythmical improvisation rather than metrical feet. As in much free verse, the lack of recurring metrical patterns lends an air of naturalness to the scene, despite the protagonist's loss of reality. The closing lines are a poignant reminder of Mephisto's description of Gretchen to Faust in the *Wald und Höhle* scene – 'Wenn ich ein Vöglein wär! so geht ihr Gesang'; (Were I a little bird so runs her song.) As is characteristic of Mephisto, nothing is as it seems. Gretchen's song lends voice to her murdered child who appropriates this symbol of freedom. The folk-like nature of the song's language, reminiscent of a fairy tale, unmetered and loosely rhymed, is a poignant reminder of 'Der König in Thule'. There Gretchen sang as a naïve child; now she is transformed into a second Ophelia whose sorrow is transformed into a perceptive madness. She describes her situation in a defamiliarized way, her loss of reality completing her isolation.

Seóirse Bodley's setting of 'Meine Mutter, die Hur'

Gretchen's song of madness has its origins in the folkfable, 'Von dem Machandelboom' (From the Juniperbush), the story of a stepmother who murders her stepson and serves him up as a meal to the father. When she hides the bones under a juniper bush, a beautiful bird arises from them to fly away to tell the tale. It bears gifts to the father and sister, kills the stepmother and turns itself back into the brother. The fable first appeared on 9 and 12 July in Achim von Arnim's *Zeitung für Einsiedler*, illustrated by the

---

[172] *HA*, 3, p.417, ll.21-29.

Hamburg writer and painter, Philipp Otto Runge (1777-1810). As early as May 1800 Jakob Grimm had sent a summary to Friedrich Karl von Savigny, the text subsequently appearing as no.47 in the Grimm brothers' *Kinder- und Hausmärchen*. The motif of the stepmother who kills her son and serves him as a meal to the father is found in stories from the Orient and antiquity; Goethe knew the story from the oral tradition.

Gretchen's song of madness is composed in irregular lines which hinge around the silence in this setting. The piano strikes up its musical representation of insanity in semiquaver octaves (bars 375-76) which are abruptly broken off by a single staccato C voiced *ssff* (bar 378). The dramatic silence these bars create leaves a tension hanging in the air as the audience are left wondering what comes next. Gretchen's opening melody, condemning the mother of her murdered child moves from middle C (bar 378) up to a high A flat (bar 380) and down to a low D (bar 381); the condemnation of her father rises a semitone higher to a *fortissimo* B flat (bar 384), its descent again answered by the closing gesture of the cathedral scene (bar 385) and poignant silence (bars 386-88). The first *piano* marking occurs at bar 388, subtly scoring the changing metres of Gretchen's lyrical lines, the tension maintained in reflective, gentle pauses (bars 396 and 401). In bars 402-408 the bird's ascent is depicted in the melodic trajectory from a high F (bar 403) to A (bars 405 and 407) to G (bar 408). The bird's flight is underscored in the higher middle range of the piano; on its final ascent in bar 408, the left hand descends into the lower bass register above which the treble soars into the higher regions of the piano to signal the bird's departure. The cycle closes with a very simple C major chord, its distance between treble and bass, as in the preceding chords (bars 409-10), a characteristic gesture of this setting.

'Wandrers Nachtlied' ('Über allen Gipfeln ist Ruh')

Goethe's lyric was conceived on the evening of 6 September 1780,[173] while the poet stood alone upon the Gickelhahn, the highest of the mountains around Illmenau.[174] Here, the poet wrote the lyric on the wall of a wooden hunting cabin, where he often spent the night. Although Goethe later dated the poem as 7 September 1783,[175] a letter to Charlotte von Stein on 6 September 1780, written at Illmenau, echoes the mood and setting of his verse:

> Auf dem Gickelhahn [...] hab' ich mich gebettet [...] um die Wüste des Städtchens....der unverbesserlichen Verworrenheit der Menschen auszuweichen [...] Es ist ein ganz reiner Himmel, und ich gehe, des Sonnenuntergangs mich zu freuen. Die Aussicht ist groß aber einfach. – Die Sonne ist unter [...] Jetzt ist die Gegend [...] so rein und ruhig, und so uninteressant, als eine große schöne Seele, wenn sie sich am wohlsten befindet. – Wenn nicht noch hie und da einige Vapeurs von den Meilern aufstiegen, wär' die ganze Szene unbeweglich.[176]

> I have lain down on the Gickelhahn [...] to avoid the incorrigible confusion of men. It is a really pure sky and I go to enjoy the sunset. The view is great but simple. When the sun is down [...] the area is [...] so pure and peaceful, and so interesting, like a great beautiful soul when feeling at its best. If some vapours from charcoal did not rise here and there, the entire scene would be motionless.

---

[173] Although composed in 1780, Goethe's verse was first published in his *Werken 1815*. Segebrecht suggests that Goethe reluctantly published the lyric after pirated versions began to appear in print after performances of Zelter's lied. There are three manuscripts, one sent to Charlotte von Stein, Herder's copy and one made by Fräulein von Göchhausen. In Charlotte von Stein's manuscript, line one is written as 'alle', line two has 'findest du' in place of 'ist', 'all' is written in line three and line four has 'Spürst' in lieu of 'Spürest'. Herder's and Fräulein von Göchhausen's copies have' Gefilden' in line two and all three editions have 'Vögel' for 'Vögelein'.

[174] Kurt Eissler suggests that the verse was written just after 8p.m.on 6 September 1780, *Goethe: A Psychoanalytic Study*, 1775-1786 (Detroit: Wayne State University Press, I, p.466.

[175] *Goethe Briefe*, 4, HA., Letter no.1505, *An Zelter* , 4 September 1831, p.442.

[176] *Goethe Briefe, WA.*, IV, 4, Letter no.1012, *An Charlotte von Stein*, 6 September 1780, pp.281-82.

Knebel's diary entry on 7 October 1780 where he writes 'Morgens schön. Mond. Goethens Verse ("Über allen Gipfeln"). Die Nacht wieder auf dem Gickelhahn' (A lovely morning. The moon. Goethe's Verse ('Über allen Gipfeln'). The night on the Gickelhahn again)[177] confirms this date. On the eve of his eighty-third birthday, Goethe returned to the Gickelhahn for the last time.[178] Berginspektor Mahr, who accompanied him on this visit, relates how moved Goethe was as he reread his verse:

> Goethe überlas diese wenigen Verse und Tränen flossen über seine Wangen. Ganz langsam zog er sein schneeweißes Taschentuch aus seinem dunkelbraunen Rock, trocknete sich die Tränen, und sprach in sanftem, wehmütigem Ton: 'Ja, warte nur, balde ruhest Du auch!' schwieg eine halbe Minute, sah nochmals durch das Fenster in den dunkeln Fichtenwald, und wendete sich dann zu mir mit den Worten: 'Nun, wollen wir wieder gehen'.[179]

> Goethe read over these few verses and tears flowed down his cheeks. Very slowly he pulled his snow-white handkerchief out of his dark-brown coat, dried his tears, and spoke in gentle, melancholic tones, 'Yes, wait, soon you too will be still!' He remained silent for half a minute, looking through the window into the dark pine forest, and turned to me with the words, 'Now, let's go again'.

At Goethe's request, the writing was renewed by Oberforstmeister von Frisch, who wrote underneath: 'Renov., den 29 Oct, 1831'. The original *Bretterhäuschen* was burned down on 11 August 1870, but was replaced soon afterwards by an exact replica with the poem engraved.

While Sternfeld does not list it in his study of Goethe's parodies, many critics trace Goethe's verse back to the following *Volkslied*:

Schlaf, Kindlein, balde!	Sleep soon, little child,
Die Vögelein singen im Walde,	The little birds sing in the woods
Sie fliegen den Wald wohl auf und nieder	They soar up in the forest and descend
Und bringen dem Kindlein die Ruhe wieder	To let children slumber once more.
Schlaf, Kindlein, schlaf![180]	Sleep, little child, sleep.

A further parallel has been found in a fragment of a Sappho poem, which opens, 'Schlummer liegt auf Bergeshöhn' (Slumber lies on the mountain tops), to which the German translator, Mähty, gave the title, 'Über allen Gipfeln ist Ruh'. Baumgart lists an additional source as the Greek lyric by Alman, which he cites in its German translation:

Schlafend liegen der Berge Gipfel und die Täler,
Uferklippen und Felsenschluchten,
Laubgezweig und alles Gewürm der schwarzen Erde,
Tiere des Bergwalds und das Volk der Bienen,
Und die Ungeheuer der dunklen Meerstiefe,
Schlaf umfängt der Vögel
Breitgefiederte Schwärme.

The mountain peaks and the vales lie sleeping
Riverbank cliffs and rocky gorges
Leafy boughs and all creeping things of the black earth,

---

[177] Hans Gerhard Gräf, *Goethe über seine Dichtungen* 3 vols (Munich: Rütten & Loening, 1967), III, p.64.

[178] *WA.*, III, 13, p.129.

[179] Boyd, I, p. 159. See *Goethe: Conversation and Encounters* ed. by David Luke and Robert Pick, (London: Oswald Wolff, 1966), J. Ch. Mahr, 27 August 1831, p.236.

[180] Boyd, I, p. 161.

Animals of the mountain woods and all bees
And the monsters of the dark ocean depths,
Sleep enfolds the flocks of
Broadwinged birds.

Despite similarities in Mähty's title and with the early *Volkslied*, Goethe's verse is not a parody: unlike Goethe's parodies, 'Wandrers Nachtlied' does not share the rhythmic structures of these early poems. Furthermore, the circumstances in which 'Wandrers Nachtlied' was composed suggest an occasional poem. In a letter to the Marchioness Branconi Goethe related the immediate afflatus he received at Illmenau and spoke of the poetry he could have written if he had been assisted by:

> ein halbduzzend Geister zu Sekretairs [...] denen man zu Pferde, bey Tafel, in dem Vorzimmer und allenfalls auch träumend dicktiren könnte.[181]

> a half dozen spirits as secretaries [...] to whom one could dictate on horseback, at table, in the anteroom and also, perhaps, while dreaming.

In the light of this confession, Goethe's lyric would not appear to be a parody, but a momentary reflection of a certain and perhaps rare experience of Nature. Unlike these early sources, 'Wandrers Nachtlied' does not merely portray a natural scene, but records a poet's intuitive comprehension of a specific reality.

In 'Wandrers Nachtlied' the stillness and silence of Nature is recreated through the movement and music of Goethe's poem. The stasis of the scene is in counterpoint with the vestigial movement underlying these images, and Goethe captures this dynamic in lines of varied metre and length. The images of tranquillity are unveiled in the first four lines, composed in iambic or trochaic feet. As the poet's eye moves from the outer scene to himself, the metre often broadens to choriambic feet. This alteration of images is mirrored through the metre, as the number of accented and unaccented syllables is varied in each line. Lines one, five, seven and eight begin with an accented foot, while lines two, three and six commence with an upbeat.

Table 3: Goethe, 'Wandrers Nachtlied'

Wandrers Nachtlied II	Rhyme scheme	The Wayfarer's Night Song II
Über allen Gipfeln	a	Over all the hill-tops
Ist Ruh,	b	It is still,
In allen Wipfeln	a	In all the tree tops
Spürest du	b	You can hardly feel
Kaum einen Hauch;	c	A breath stirring.
Die Vögelein schweigen im Walde.	d	The little birds are silent in the forest.
Warte nur, balde	d	Wait! Soon
Ruhest du auch.	c	You too will be still

Lines one and six have three stresses, line two has one, while the remaining lines contain two beats. Through this rhythmic arrangement Goethe underscores his pacified poem with movement. Although composed in free form, the use of end-rhyme, *ababcddc*, assonance and changing metrical patterns lends a rich musicality to his poem.

'Wandrers Nachtlied' captures the serenity of the natural scene, which Goethe experienced on the evening of 6 September 1780. In three simple images the poet relates the tranquillity on the hill-tops, the stillness of the tree-tops; the silence of the birds[182] in

---

181 *WA.*, IV, 4, Letter no.1028, *An Frau Marquise Branconi*, 16 October 1780, p.320.
182 In the early manuscripts of the poems, Goethe wrote 'Vögel' in lieu of 'Vögelein'. the diminutive, first appeared around 1814 in musical renditions of the poem. The diminutive recalls the style of a *Volkslied* and also intensifies the musicality of the poem.

the forest, and the final lines are addressed to man: 'Warte nur, balde /Ruhest du auch'. By listing three aspects of the natural scene, moving nearer to himself with each step, the poet implies how man is part of this chain. The poet reinforces this connection through his language, where the peace of Nature (line two) is repeated in relation to man (line eight). The chiastic construction reinforces this parity and reveals an extraordinary intimate permeation of self and World. Goethe's sequence also insinuates the inner processes of the mind. By presenting an entire scene through a few salient features, the poet relates the scene as he perceives it and expresses, as it awakens, his poetic response. Although Goethe's language is simple, it is rich in association. The simplicity and concreteness of imagery is highly symbolic and alludes to the poet's experience of Nature as Divine.[183] The telescoping of images reinforces the primordial Unity in Nature, and the poet experiences the self as cradled in its embracing Presence. In 'Wandrers Nachtlied' Goethe advances through the individual phenomena to the idea whose symbolic representation is the ultimate objective.

Many critics have pondered over the meaning of the verb 'ruhen' in Goethe's closing couplet. In conversation with Chancellor von Müller on 6 June 1830, Goethe used the term in relation to his own death, claiming: 'Ich bin alt genug, um Ruhe zu wünschen' (I am old enough to desire repose). In 'Wandrers Nachtlied', Goethe's use of the verb 'ruhen' to suggest death is closely linked concatenated to his attitude to death. By using the verb 'to rest', the poet does not imply inactivity and calling a halt to a process of development. Rest is linked with life; it alludes to the concept of circularity, as it effects regeneration. The poem portrays the capacity of art to grasp the changeful, death-bound beauty of life, while simultaneously surrendering any claim on its permanence. In a letter to Lavater, dated 3 November 1780, Goethe speaks of our return to Nature in death:

> Die Zeit kommt doch bald, wo wir zerstreut werden, in die Elemente zurückkehren, aus denen wir genommen sind[184]

> The time approaches when we will be scattered and return to the elements out of which we evolved

and in 'Wandrers Nachtlied', he alludes to death as a function of the never-ending process of life. For Goethe life and death form a unity after the fashion of polar opposition; they are two functions which can only exist side by side and are interwoven with each other. Death is an aspect of living and within every being, at all levels of existence, life and death coexist. In 'Wandrers Nachtlied', Goethe captures the tension between these countervailing forces in line five, where he writes 'kaum einen Hauch' (hardly a breath). The image implies death and yet by introducing the word 'kaum' (hardly), Goethe suggests signs of life. The noun 'Hauch' intensifies this association, for it suggests breath at its minimum and so evokes both life and death. For Goethe, the drive to return to equilibrium connects death and rebirth. In *Hermann und Dorothea*, he relates how the picture of death should point man back to life and teach him to be active. He echoes these words in the prose hymn to Nature (1781), where life is the loveliest invention of Nature, 'und der Tod ist ihr Kunstgriff, viel Leben zu haben' (and death is her ploy to live fully).[185] Similarly, in 'Wandrers Nachtlied', new existence comes from the contemplation of death. Goethe's experience of death reminds the poet that he must go beyond and that is the essential ingredient of progress and of life. As Nature is the source of his being, the poet recognizes it as his limit.

---

[183] Elizabeth M. Wilkinson's analysis of the lyric contradicts this statement, where she writes: 'There is not a simile, not a metaphor, not a symbol. Three brief simple statements of fact are followed by a plain assertion for the future'. See 'Goethe's Poetry', *German Life and Letters*, 2(1949), pp.316-29.

[184] *WA.*, IV, 3, Letter no.1035, *An Lavater*, 3 November 1780, p.329.

[185] Fragment über die Natur, HA., 13, p.46.

Seóirse Bodley's Setting of 'Wandrers Nachtlied'

Bodley's 'Wandrers Nachtlied' was composed on 26 April 2003 to mark the launch of my first monograph, *Schubert's Goethe Settings*,[186] which took place at the Goethe-Institut Ireland on 6 May 2003. Following a short recital of three of Schubert's Goethe settings – 'Ganymed', 'Der König in Thule' and 'Der Fischer' – performed by Aylish Kerrigan (mezzo soprano) and Seóirse Bodley (piano), with alternating recitations of the Goethe lyrics by Peter Jankowsky, the setting was premiered by the Lieder duo at the recital's close. The lied was beautifully rendered by Kerrigan and it also received a very sensitive performance by Anne Woodworth (mezzo-soprano) and Caroline Senior (piano) at the Festival for New Music, Waterford on 31 January 2005. Another significant performance was the rendition by Sylvia O'Brien (soprano) and Seóirse Bodley (piano), as a fitting encore to their recital of Faust settings on 20 April 2012.

On a trip to Weimar we took a bus to Illmenau and a taxi up to the small Museum on the Gickelhahn in order to revisit the place where Goethe's poem was conceived. The most remarkable aspect of the visit was the experience of absolute stillness on the Gickelhahn over two centuries later – an experience which influenced Bodley's setting of the poem.[187] The Lento setting, dynamic range from *piano* to triple *piano*, and sparse piano accompaniment evoke the sense of quietude in which Goethe's scene is clothed. As in Goethe's lyric where the stasis of Nature indicates a state of equilibrium between the internal and external world, the song should be sung in a very inward manner, almost to oneself, the audience becoming onlookers much like Berginspektor Mahr as he bore witness to the 82-year old poet's contemplation of the scene.

The setting has its origins in a twelve-note row with three additional moveable notes:

Musical Example 3: Bodley, 'Wandrers Nachtlied', Basic Series

The three-bar piano introduction arises from the basic series 1 (including the three moveable notes (which underscore bars 4-5); the piano accompaniment has its origins in inversion 1 in the accompaniment (bars 6-8); all 15 notes of retrograde 2 (bars 9-12); retrograde inversion 8 (bars 13-16) and all 15 notes of the basic series 9 (bars 16-21). Bodley's melody arises from the basic series 1 (bars 4-10) and retrograde inversion 7 (bars 13-18), where the three moveable notes – C, F and G (bars 16-17) are voiced before the final F sharp on 'auch'.

Unlike the sustained lines of Schubert's setting, Bodley deliberately sets the text in disjointed, yet sonorous, vocal lines which intensify the musical expression of Goethe's poem. As much of the poem's meaning comes from the musicality of its sparse diction, much of the music's meaning arises through the laconic texture of Bodley's setting. An example of this is found in the deliberate placing of rests within key textual phrases 'kaum einen Hauch (with its mirrored diphtongs in bar 9) and 'Ruhest du auch' (bars 17-18), and in particular the very different (poetic) cadences to which those rests give rise when immediately placed before 'Hauch' (bar 9) and 'auch' (bar 18). Although deliberately disjointed, this musical gesture subtly points the end-rhyme in these lines,

---

[186] Lorraine Byrne Bodley, *Schubert's Goethe Settings* (Ashgate, 2003).

[187] The composer's immediately apprehension of the poetic experience was also informed by a similar epiphany (and subsequent artistic expression) in his own life. See Gareth Cox, Seóirse Bodley (Dublin: Field Day Publications, 2010), pp.144-45.

which Bodley mirrors in the musical rhyme, F sharp. Through such gestures the composer compensates for the loss of poetic music, perhaps even enhancing its musicality and embodied poetic meaning. A second example of very subtle text setting is found in the poet's telescoping of natural images from the mountain tops to the poetic self which is subtly observed through the composer's circling of pitches around 'D'. The natural summit of Goethe's scene is musically observed by placing the vocal climax on 'Gipfeln', D sharp, in the singer's opening bar. As the poet surveys his surroundings moving closer to the poetic self, Bodley's vocal line gradually descends from 'D sharp' on 'Gipfeln' to a sustained 'D' on 'Ruh' (bar 6), falling from 'D' – 'D flat' on 'allen Wipfeln' (bars 4-8) to 'C' on the first syllable of 'Vög'lein' (bar 12). Through this flattened contour, the chromatic reversal C-D flat (on 'Vög'lein' bar 12) rising again to 'D' 'nur balde' (bars 15-16) is thematically well prepared. Through both musical gestures the composer endorses the poetic narrative while avoiding a sense of superficial parallelism (which Schoenberg might have dismissed as 'primitive').

The recitative-like piano accompaniment in the opening bars of Goethe's text and the spare texture of the accompaniment through the song underscores the poet's response to the stillness of Nature, the complete receptivity between Nature and Man, and interdependence of all phenomena. The musical movement in the piano interludes (bars 10-12, 14 and 16) recognizes how in nature this interstice is a reality in action, still and intensely a piece of life. The immanent action of the scene is heralded by ascending quavers A to B flat (bars 14-15) which mark a momentary vista into the nature of experience, whereby the poet calmly recognizes the certainty of his eventual demise.[188] Once again, the poet's embodiment of this truth in the closing couplet is voiced in deliberately disjointed lines, whereby the poet's parting words 'warte', 'nur', 'balde' 'ruhest du' 'auch' are intensified by the preceding rests in bars 14, 15, 16, 17 and 18 respectively. Here, once again, Bodley is masterful in his enhancement of the psychological. In a very subtle way, the rests symbolize the poet's fusion with the concrete vacuum in Nature, mirrored within himself, which leads him to the recognition of the temporal in the timeless, the finite in the infinite. This 'disappearance of the ego' through a rare experience of the creative void justifies from beginning to end Bodley's belief that the song should be sung in a very inward manner. And Goethe's resounding silence can be heard in the reverbant echo of the piano postlude.

---

[188] Goethe's reaction to his verse on his final visit to Illmenau supports this reading of the poem. See Goethe's conversation with Soret on 8 March 1830, *Goethe im Gespräch*, ed. by Eduard Korrodi (Switzerland: Maresse Verlag, 1994), pp.503-504.

Mignon und der Harfner

Song cycle for Soprano, Baritone and Piano

Poems: Johann Wolfgang von Goethe
Music: Seóirse Bodley

Dedicated to Rolf Stehle

Accidentals apply to the note they prefix for the rest of the bar
at the same pitch only: they do not apply to other octaves.

1. An die Türen will ich schleichen

Johann Wolfgang von Goethe

Seóirse Bodley

wird   Nah -   rung

rei - chen,   Und   ich

wer -   de   wei -   ter   gehn.

Je - der wird sich glück - lich schei- nen

Wenn mein Bild vor ihm er - scheint,

Ei - ne Trä - ne wird er

wei - nen, Und ich weiß nicht was er weint.

2. Heiß mich nicht reden

ist— mir Pflicht;—

Ich möch - te dir mein

gan - zes Inn - - re

81

zei - - gen,   Al -lein das   Schick - sal

87

will es   nicht._____   Zur

pp   *mp*

93

rech - ten   Zeit._____   ver - treibt der   Son - - ne

99   *mp*

Lauf   Die fin - stre   Nacht,_____   und sie muß sich er-

sfp

hel - len; Der har - te Fels___ schließt sei -nen

Bu - - - sen auf___ Miß - gönnt der

Er - de nicht die tief - ver - borg - nen Quel -

- len. Ein je - der

sucht_____ im Arm des Freun - -

- - - - des Ruh,_____

— Dort kann die Brust in Kla -

- - - gen sich er - gie - - -

ßen; Al - lein ein

Schwur___ drückt_____ mir___ die

Lip - pen___ zu___ Und nur ein Gott ver - mag sie

auf - zu - schlie - ßen.

3. Wer nie sein Brot mit Tränen aß

Der kennt euch nicht, ihr himm - li - schen

Mäch - te.

Ihr führt ins Le - ben uns hin - ein,

Ihr laßt den Ar - men schul - dig wer - den, Dann ü - ber -laßt ihr

ihn der Pein; Denn al - le Schuld rächt sich auf

Er - - - - - den.

4. Kennst du das Land?

Myr - te still_____ und hoch der Lor - beer steht.

Kennst du es wohl? Da- hin! Da- hin!_____

_____ Möcht ich mit dir,_____ o mein Ge - lieb - ter,

(stonily)

bil - der stehn und sehn mich an:___ Was hat man

dir, du arm-es Kind, ge - tan? Kennst du es wohl?

Da - hin! Da-hin! Möcht ich mit dir, o mein Be

schüt - zer, ziehn.

Kennst du den Berg und sei - nen

Wol - ken - steg? Das Maul - tier

sucht im Ne - bel sei - nen Weg, In

251
Höh - len wohnt der Dra - chen al - te

253
Brut, Es stürzt der Fels und

255
ü - - ber ihn die

256
Flut. Kennst du ihn wohl? Da

hin! Da-hin!   geht un - ser Weg!____   o Va - ter,

laß   uns   ziehn!

sempre diminuendo

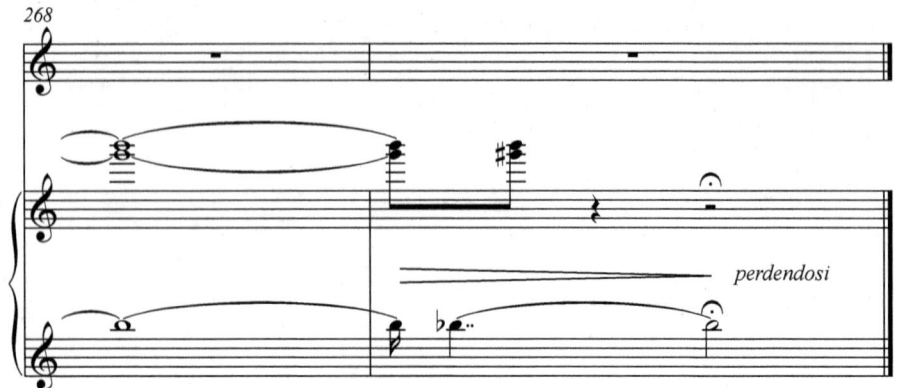

perdendosi

5. Wer sich der Einsamkeit ergibt

Und kann ich nur___ ein - mal Recht ein - sam sein,___

___ Dann bin ich___ nicht___ al - lein.___

Es___ schleicht ein Lie - ben -

299

- der lau - schend sacht,_____ Ob sei -ne Freun -din

303

al - lein? So ü - ber - schleicht____ bei Tag und Nacht___

306

Mich Ein - sam - en_____ die Pein,_

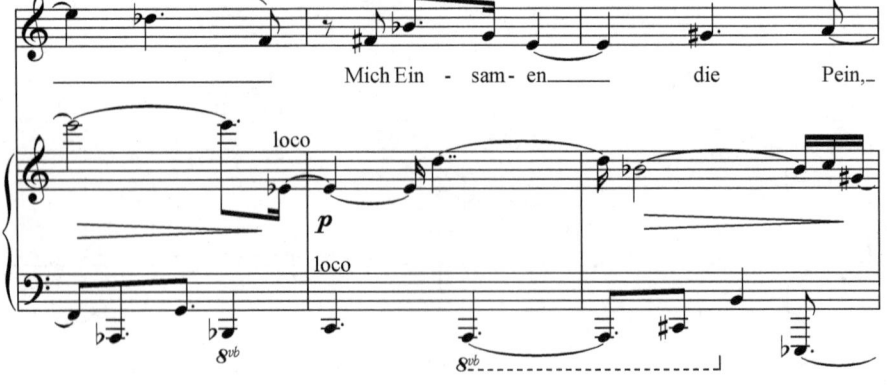

6. So laßt mich scheinen bis ich werde

mir das wei-ße Kleid

nicht aus! Ich ei - le,

von der schö - nen Er - de Hin-ab in je - nes

357
Blick, Ich las - se____ dann die rei - ne

360
Hül - - le,____ Den Gür - tel____ und den Kranz zu-

363
rück.____

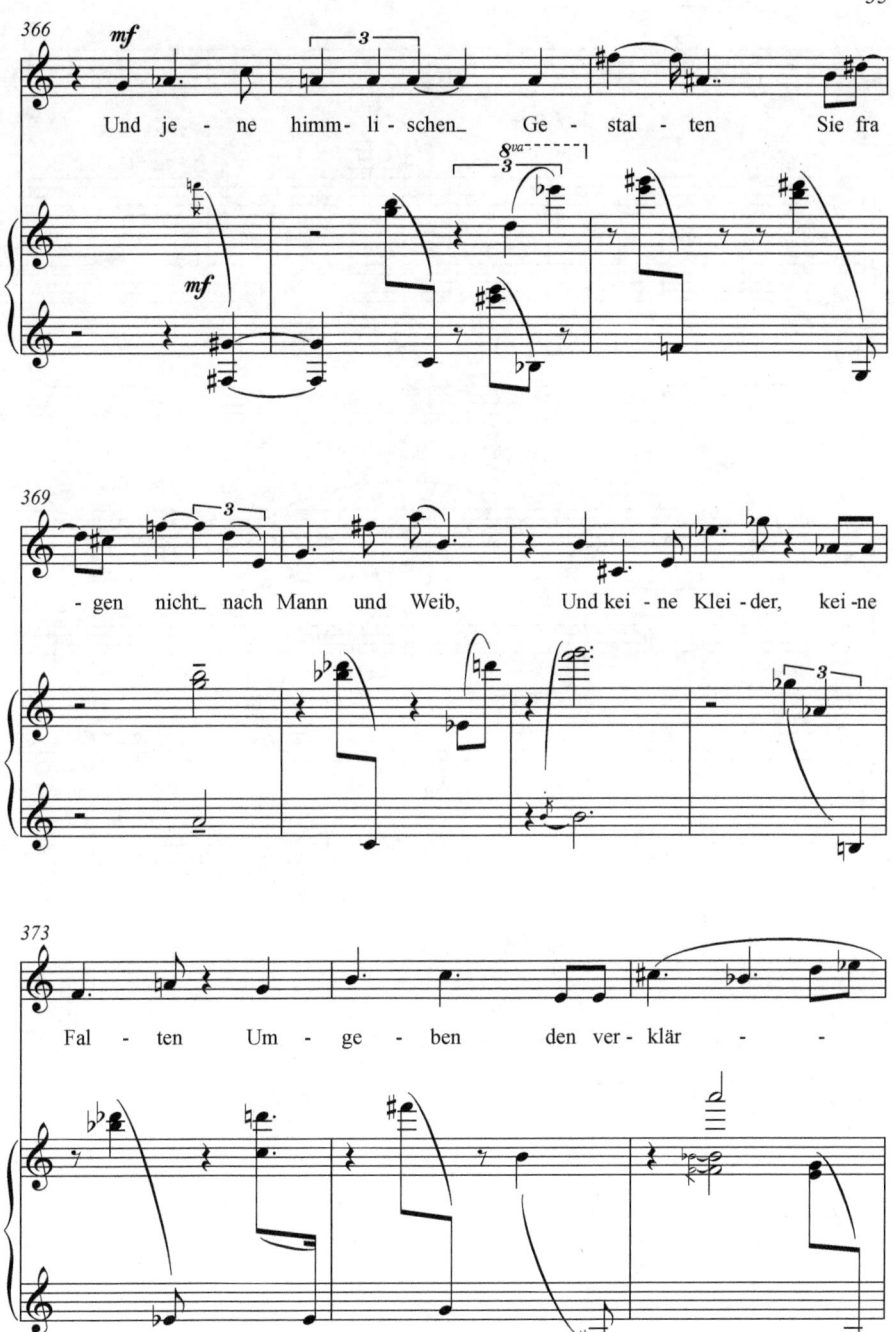

Und je - ne himm- li - schen Ge - stal - ten Sie fra

- gen nicht nach Mann und Weib, Und kei - ne Klei - der, kei - ne

Fal - ten Um - ge - ben den ver - klär - -

ten Leib.   Zwar

lebt'   ich   oh -ne   Sorg   und

Mü –   he   Doch   fühlt'   ich   tie - fen

Schmerz_____ ge - nung.   Vor

Kum - mer al - tert ich_____ zu frü - - he,

Macht_____ mich auf e - - wig

wie - - - der jung._____

7. Nur wer die Sehnsucht kennt

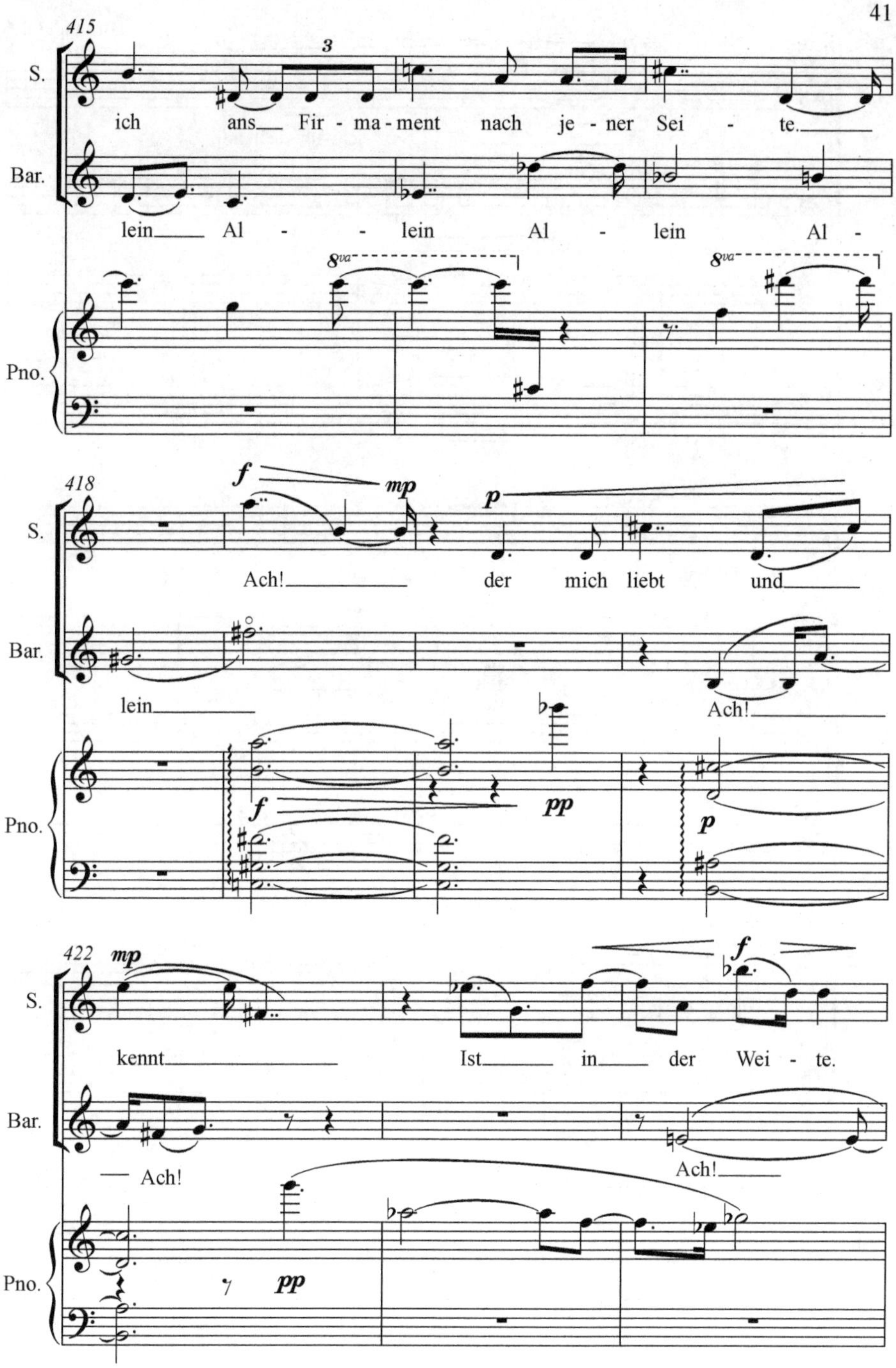

ich ans Fir - ma - ment nach je - ner Sei - te.

lein Al - lein Al - lein Al -

Ach! der mich liebt und

lein Ach!

kennt Ist in der Wei - te.

Ach! Ach!

42

44

Gretchen

Song cycle for Soprano, Mezzo-soprano, Choir and Piano

Poems: Johann Wolfgang von Goethe
Music: Seóirse Bodley

Dedicated to Prof. Nicholas Boyle
World-renowned authority on Goethe
Schroeder Professor of German, Magdalene College Cambridge

Every accidental applies to the note it prefixes and lasts for the rest of the bar at the same pitch.

Where there are two parts on a bass stave an 8vb line refers to both parts.

Johann Wolfgang von Goethe

1. Der König in Thule

Seóirse Bodley

Städt' im Reich,___ Gönnt' al - les sei - nem Er - ben, Den Be -

cher___nicht zu - gleich. Er saß beim Kö-nigs

mah-le, Die Rit - ter um ihn her, Auf Hoh - em Vä - ter Saa - le, Dort___

auf dem Schloß am Meer.

Dort stand der al - te

Ze - cher, Trank letz - te Le - bens glut, - Und

warf den heil' - gen Be - cher Hin - un - ter in die

Flut.

Er sah ihn

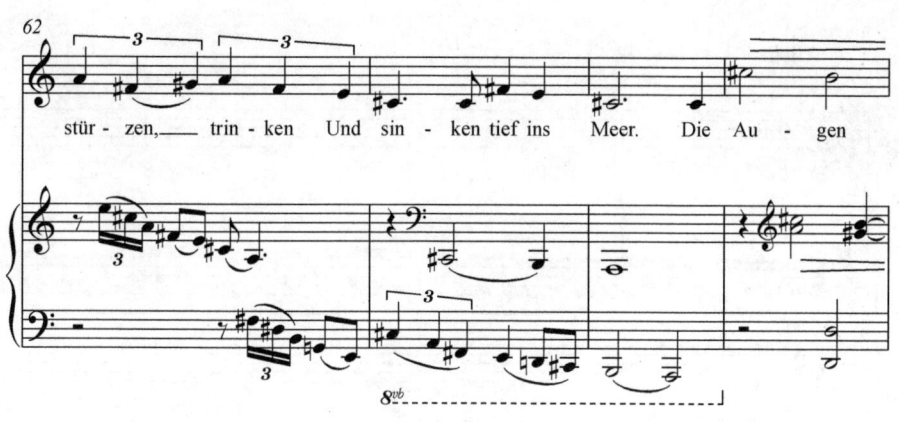

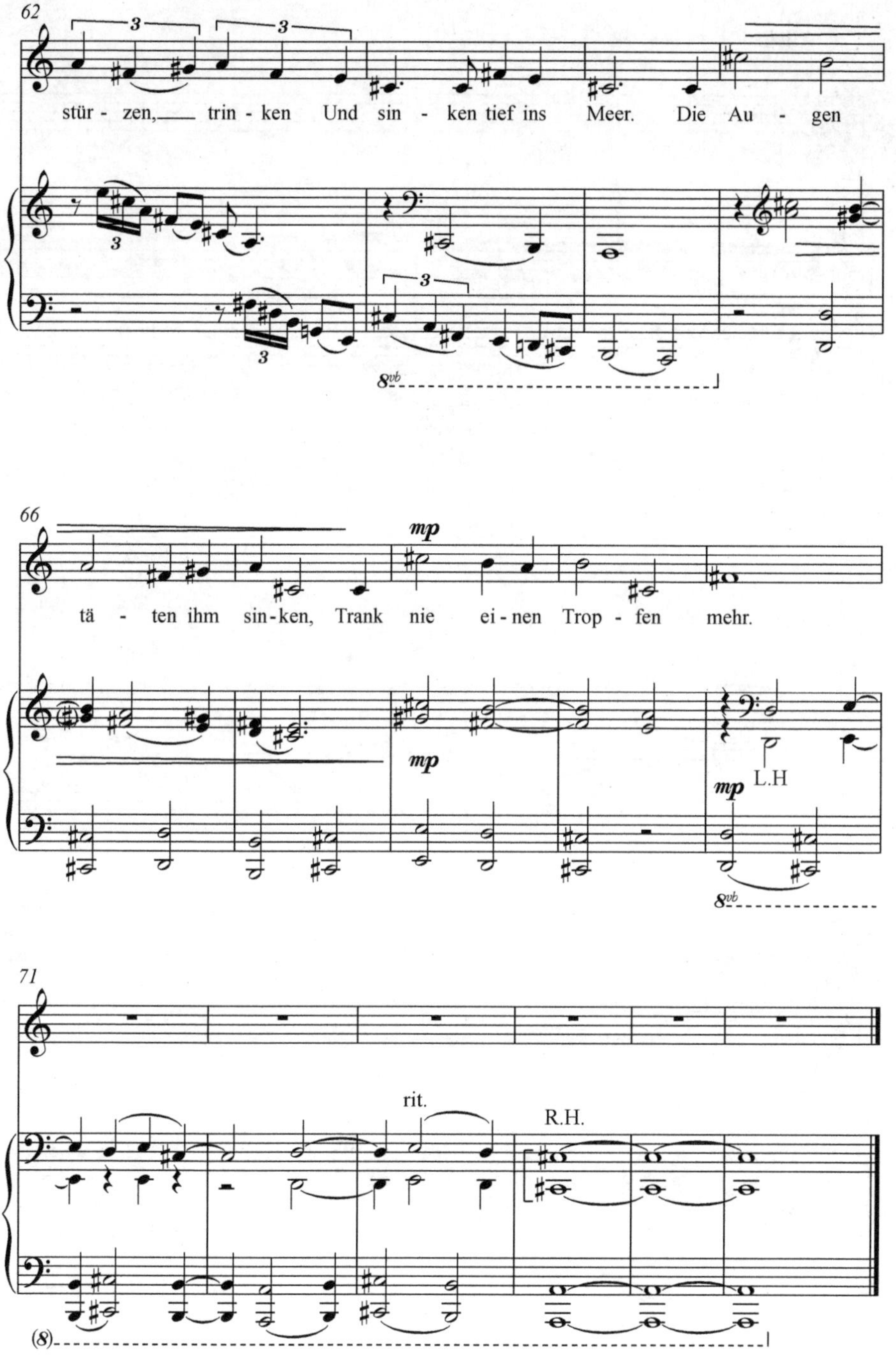
62
stür - zen, trin - ken Und sin - ken tief ins Meer. Die Au - gen
8vb
66
mp
tä - ten ihm sin - ken, Trank nie ei - nen Trop - fen mehr.
mp
mp
L.H
8vb
71
rit.
R.H.
(8)

2. Gretchen am Spinnrade

Herz ist schwer, Ich fin - de sie

nim - mer Und nim - - - -

mer - - mehr.___

Wo ich

ihn_____ nicht hab' Ist mir das Grab,

Die gan - ze__ Welt Ist mir_____ ver -

gällt.

101 *mp*

Mein ar - mer Kopf Ist___

102

mir___ ver - rückt, Mein ar - mer Sinn Ist mir zer -

104

stückt.

mf

106 *mf*

Mei - ne Ruh' ist hin, Mein Herz ist schwer,

Ich fin - de sie nim - mer Ich fin - de sie nim - mer Und nim -

- mer - mehr.

un poco più mosso

Nach

ihm nur schau' ich Zum Fen - ster hin - aus, Nach

ihm nur geh ich Aus dem Haus. Sein

ho - her Gang, Sein' ed - le Ge - stalt, Sei-nes Mun - des

Lä-cheln, Sei-ner Au - gen Ge - walt, Und sei - ner Re - de

Zau - ber - fluß, Sein Hän - de-druck,

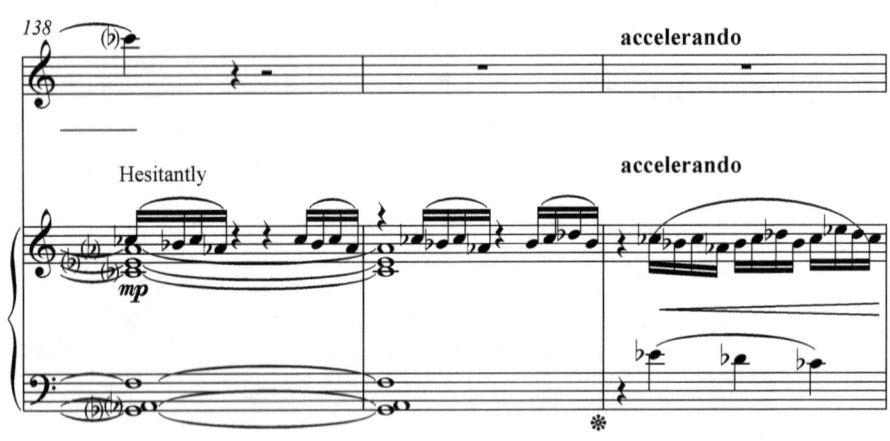

Und küs-sen ihn So wie ich wollt', An sei - - nen

Küs - sen Ver - ge - - - hen, ver -

ge - hen sollt'!

auf zu dei - nes Soh - nes Tod. Zum Va - ter blickst du,

Und Seuf - zer schickst du Hin - auf um sein' und

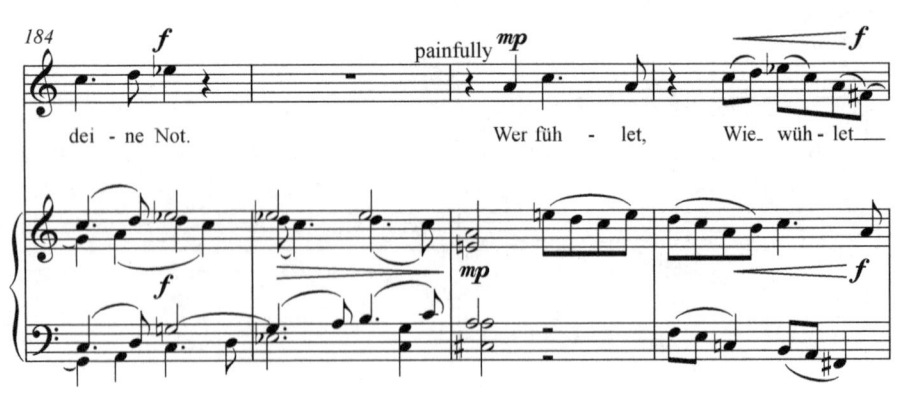

dei - ne Not. Wer füh - let, Wie wüh - let,

Der Schmerz mir ___ im Ge- bein? Was mein arm - es Herz hier bang- et,

more intensely

___ Was es zit - tert, was ver lan - get, Weißt nur du, nur du al - lein! ___

tearfully

Wo - hin ich im-mer ge - he Wie weh, wie

weh, wie we - he Wird mir im Bu - sen hier!

Ich bin ach kaum al - lei - ne, Ich

wein', ich wein', ich wei - ne, Das Herz zer - bricht in mir.

Die Scher-ben vor mei - nem Fen-ster Be

taut' ich mit Trä - nen, ach! _____ Als ich am früh - en Mor-gen

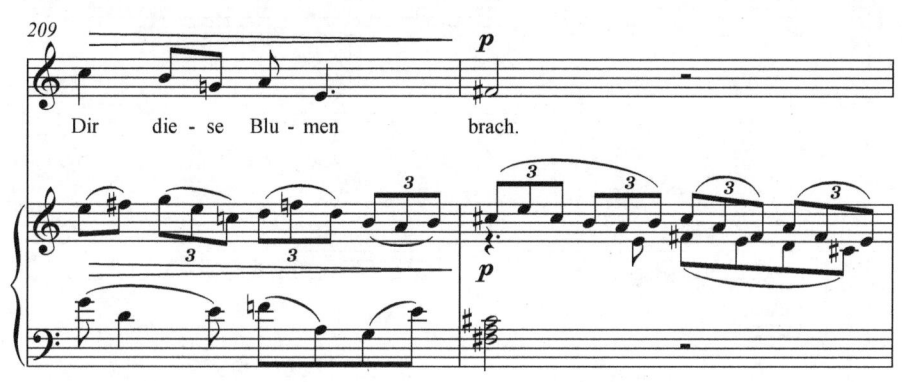

Dir die - se Blu - men brach.

more brightly

Schien hell in mei - ne Kam-mer Die Son - ne früh her -

4. Domszene

Gret - - - chen! Wo steht dein

Kopf? In dei - nem Her - zen,

Wel - che Mis - se - tat?

Bet'st du für dei - ner Mut- ter___ See - le? die Durch dich zur

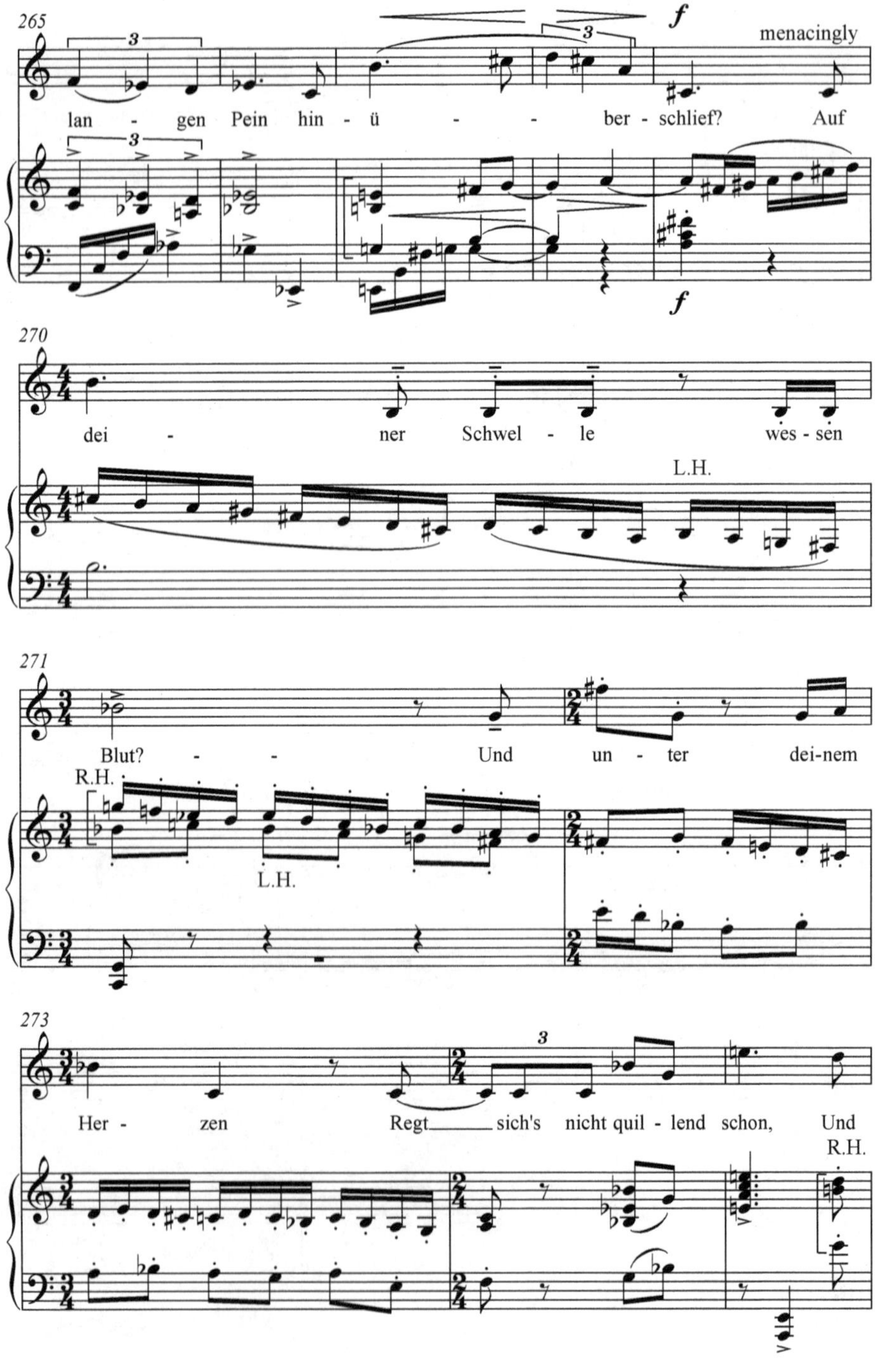
265
menacingly
lan - gen Pein hin - ü - - ber - schlief? Auf
270
dei - ner Schwel - le wes - sen
L.H.
271
Blut? - - Und un - ter dei-nem
R.H.
L.H.
273
Her - zen Regt sich's nicht quil - lend schon, Und
R.H.

*Each choral entry should be sung in a threatening manner.

ff *Gretchen* (increasingly perturbed)

306

Wär' ich hier_____ weg! Mir

R.H.

L.H.

309

ist als ob die Or-gel mir Den A - tem ver-setz - te

313

Chor
f

Ge -sang_____mein Herz. Im_ Tief-sten lö - s'te. Ju-dex_ er - go_

319

cum_ se de - bit, Quid-quid la - tet ad - pa - re-bit,_____ Nil in-ul-tum re-ma

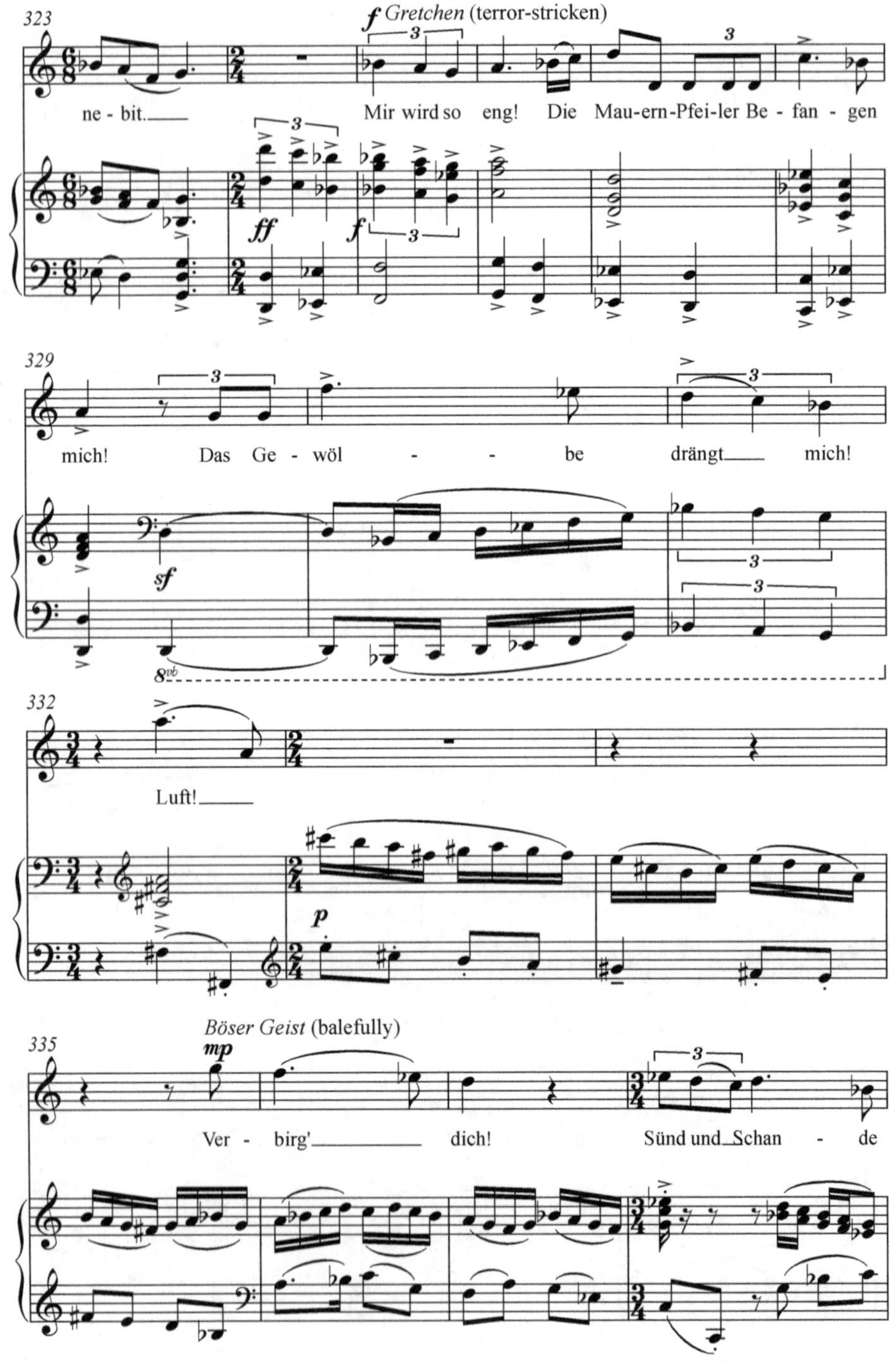
323
f Gretchen (terror-stricken)
ne - bit.
Mir wird so eng! Die Mau-ern-Pfei-ler Be - fan - gen
ff
f
329
mich! Das Ge - wöl - - be drängt mich!
sf
8vb
332
Luft!
p
335
Böser Geist (balefully)
mp
Ver - birg' dich! Sünd und Schan - de

357
rei - chen, Schau-ert's den Rei- nen. Weh!_____

362 Chor
pp
Quid sum mi - ser   tunc dic tu- rus?   Quem pa - tro - num   ro - ga-tu - rus?

366
ff *Gretchen* (dramatically)
Nach - - bar -

368
in!   Eu - er   Fläsch - - - chen!

5. Meine Mutter, die Hur

(Gretchen's song of madness from the prison scene)

*These rests should be filled with tension.

Wandrers Nachtlied

Song for Mezzo-soprano and Piano

Poem: Johann Wolfgang von Goethe
Music: Seóirse Bodley

Wandrers Nachtlied II

Über allen Gipfeln
Ist Ruh,
In allen Wipfeln
Spürest du
Kaum einen Hauch;
Die Vögelein schweigen im Walde.
Warte nur, balde
Ruhest du auch.

Johann Wolfgang von Goethe

The Wayfarer's Night Song II

Over all the hill-tops
It is still,
In all the tree tops
You can hardly feel
A breath stirring.
The little birds are silent in the forest.
Wait! Soon
You too will be still.

Translation: Lorraine Byrne Bodley

Accidentals apply to the note they prefix for the rest of the bar
at the same pitch only: they do not apply to other octaves.

Wandrers Nachtlied

for Lorraine

Johann Wolfgang von Goethe

Seóirse Bodley

Die Vög' - lein schwei - gen im

Wal - de. War - te nur,

bal - de Ru - hest du

auch.

APPENDIX 1

MIGNON UND DER HARFNER   Johann Wolfgang von Goethe

An die Türen will ich schleichen

An die Türen will ich schleichen,
Still und sittsam will ich stehn,
Frommer Hand wird Nahrung reichen,
Und ich werde weiter gehn.
Jeder wird sich glücklich scheinen
Wenn mein Bild vor ihm erscheint,
Eine Träne wird er weinen,
Und ich weiß nicht was er weint.

I will steal up to people's doors
I will stand piously and respectably,
Charitable hands will offer me food,
And I will wander on.
Every one will consider himself fortunate
When my image appears before him,
He will shed a tear,
And I do not know why he weeps.

Heiß mich nicht reden

Heiß mich nicht reden, heiß mich schweigen,
Denn mein Geheimnis ist mir Pflicht;
Ich möchte dir mein ganzes Innre zeigen,
Allein das Schicksal will es nicht.

Bid me not speak, bid me be silent,
For it is my duty to keep my secret.
I would like to show you my whole heart,
But my destiny does not allow it.

Zur rechten Zeit vertreibt der Sonne Lauf
Die finstre Nacht, und sie muß sich erhellen,

The circling sun in due season dispels
The dark night and light must take its place;

Der harte Fels schließt seinen Busen auf,
Mißgönnt der Erde nicht die tiefverborgnen Quellen.

The hard rock opens its bosom
And bestows its deep-hidden waters to the earth.

Ein jeder sucht im Arm des Freundes Ruh,

Every man seeks repose in the arms of a friend

Dort kann die Brust in Klagen sich ergießen;

Where he can pour out his heart in lamentation;

Allein ein Schwur drückt mir die Lippen zu
Und nur ein Gott vermag sie aufzuschließen.

Alone, a solemn oath seals my lips,
And only a god can open them.

Wer nie sein Brot mit Tränen aß

Wer nie sein Brot mit Tränen aß,

He who has never eaten his bread mixed with tears,

Wer nie die kummervollen Nächte
Auf seinem Bette weinend saß,
Der kennt euch nicht, ihr himmlischen Mächte.

He who has never through nights of anguish,
Sat weeping on his bed,
Such a man does not know you, you heavenly Powers.

Ihr führt ins Leben uns hinein,
Ihr laßt den Armen schuldig werden,

You lead us into life,
And by your will, poor wretches, we become guilty,

Dann überlaßt ihr ihn der Pein;
Denn alle Schuld rächt sich auf Erden.

And then are delivered over to suffering;
For all guilt is atoned on earth.

Kennst du das Land?

Kennst du das Land? wo die Zitronen blühn,

Im dunkeln Laub die Gold-Orangen glühn,

Ein sanfter Wind vom blauen Himmel weht,
Die Myrte still und hoch der Lorbeer steht.

Kennst du es wohl?
                        Dahin! Dahin!
Möcht ich mit dir, o mein Geliebter, ziehn!

Kennst du das Haus? auf Säulen ruht sein
Dach,
Es glänzt der Saal, es schimmert das Gemach,
Und Marmorbilder stehn und sehn mich an:

Was hat man dir, du armes Kind, getan?
Kennst du es wohl?
                        Dahin! Dahin!
Möcht ich mit dir, o mein Beschützer, ziehn.

Kennst du den Berg und seinen Wolkensteg?

Das Maultier sucht im Nebel seinen Weg,
In Höhlen wohnt der Drachen alte Brut,
Es stürzt der Fels und über ihn die Flut:

Kennst du ihn wohl?
                        Dahin! Dahin!
Geht unser Weg! o Vater, laß uns ziehn!

Do you know the land where the lemon-
trees blossom,
Where the golden oranges glow in the dark
foliage,
A soft wind falls from the blue sky,
The myrtle stands silent and the laurel is
tall?
Do you know it perhaps?
It is there, there that I would like to go with
you, my beloved.

Do you know the house? Its roof rests on
columns,
The hall gleams, the room glistens,
And the marble statues stand and gaze at
me:
'What have they done to you, poor child?'
Do you know it perhaps?
It is there, there that I would like to go with
you, my protector.

Do you know the mountain and its cloudy
path?
The mule seeks its way through the mists;
In caves the ancient brood of dragons dwell;
The crag falls sheer and the cataract
tumbles over it;
Do you know it perhaps?
It is there, there
our way leads. Oh, father, let us go!

Wer sich der Einsamkeit ergibt

Wer sich der Einsamkeit ergibt,
Ach! der ist bald allein;
Ein jeder lebt, ein jeder liebt
Und läßt ihn seiner Pein.
Ja! laßt mich meiner Qual!
Und kann ich nur einmal
Recht einsam sein,
Dann bin ich nicht allein.

Es schleicht ein Liebender lauschend sacht,

Ob seine Freundin allein?
So überschleicht bei Tag und Nacht
Mich Einsamen die Pein,

Mich Einsamen die Qual.
Ach werd' ich erst einmal
Einsam im Grabe sein,
Da läßt sie mich allein!

He who devotes himself to solitude
Alas, is soon alone.
Everybody lives, everybody loves,
And leaves him to his sorrow.
Yes! Leave me to my torment,
And if I once succeed
In finding real solitude
Then I will not be alone.

A lover creeps up softly and stands listening
to find out
Whether his sweetheart is alone.
And so, day and night
Sorrow and suffering steal stealthily upon
me
In all my solitude,
But when I finally attain
Solitude in the grave,
At last it will leave me alone.

So laßt mich scheinen

So laßt mich scheinen bis ich werde,

Zieht mir das weiße Kleid nicht aus!
Ich eile, von der schönen Erde
Hinab in jenes feste Haus.

Dort ruh ich eine kleine Stille,
Dann öffnet sich der frische Blick,
Ich lasse dann die reine Hülle,
Den Gürtel und den Kranz zurück.

Und jene himmlischen Gestalten
Sie fragen nicht nach Mann und Weib,
Und keine Kleider, keine Falten
Umgeben den verklärten Leib.

Zwar lebt' ich ohne Sorg und Mühe
Doch fühlt' ich tiefen Schmerz genung.
Vor Kummer altert ich zu frühe,
Macht mich auf ewig wieder jung!

Nur wer die Sehnsucht kennt

Nur wer die Sehnsucht kennt,
Weiß was ich leide!
Allein und abgetrennt
Von aller Freude,
Seh ich ans Firmament
Nach jener Seite.
Ach! der mich liebt und kennt
Ist in der Weite.
Es schwindet mir, es brennt
Mein Eingeweide.
Nur wer die Sehnsucht kennt,
Weiß was ich leide!

So let me appear (like an angel) until I become (one):
Do not strip me of this white robe!
I hasten from the joys of earth
Down to that house so fast and firm.

There will I rest in peace a while,
Then I shall see with new eyes,
Then I will cast aside my pure chrysalis.
Leaving both wreath and garment behind.

For all those glorious heavenly figures,
Will not ask whether I am man or woman,
No garments long or draperies fine
Will envelop my body, now transformed.

I lived indeed untouched by care.
And yet I felt my share of deep sorrow.
Suffering has made me old too soon,
Now make me young forever more!

Only those who know what longing is
Can know what I suffer!
Alone and cut off
From all joy,
I keep gazing over yonder
Into heaven's demesne.
Alas! He who loves me and knows me
Is far away.
I feel giddy,
I am on fire inside.
Only those who know what longing is
Can know what I suffer!

Translations: Lorraine Byrne Bodley

APPENDIX 2

GRETCHEN. SONGS FROM GOETHE'S *FAUST 1*

Der König in Thule (1774)
Faust 1, ll.2759-82

The King in Thule

Es war ein König in Thule,
Gar treu bis an das Grab,
Dem sterbend seine Buhle
Einen goldnen Becher gab.

Once there was a king in Thule,
Faithful to the grave,
To whom his lady as she died
Gave a golden wine-cup.

Es ging ihm nichts darüber,
Er leert' ihn jeden Schmaus;
Die Augen gingen ihm über,
So oft er trank daraus.

He valued it above everything,
He drained it at every feast,
And each time he drank from it
Tears came to his eyes.

Und als er kam zu sterben,
Zählt' er seine Städt' im Reich,
Gönnt' alles seinem Erben,
Den Becher nicht zugleich.

And when he came to die
He numbered the cities of his kingdom
And withheld nothing from his heir
Except only the cup.

Er saß beim Königsmahle,
Die Ritter um ihn her,
Auf hohem Väter-Saale,
Dort auf dem Schloß am Meer.

He sat at the royal banquet,
With his knights all around him,
In his high ancestral hall
Up there in the castle by the sea.

Dort stand der alte Zecher,
Trank letzte Lebensglut,
Und warf den heiligen Becher
Hinunter in die Flut.

There the old toper stood,
Drinking life's last glow,
And he threw the sacred cup
Down into the waves.

Er sah ihn stürzen, trinken
Und sinken tief ins Meer,
Die Augen täten ihm sinken
Trank nie einen Tropfen mehr.

He saw it fall and fill with water
And sink right into the sea,
Then did his eyelids droop,
And never another drop he drank.

Gretchen am Spinnrade
(1774/75)
Faust 1, ll.3374-413

Gretchen at the Spinning Wheel

Meine Ruh' ist hin,
Mein Herz ist schwer,
Ich finde sie nimmer
Und nimmermehr.

My heart's heavy
I have lost my peace of mind
And I'll never never
Find it again.

Wo ich ihn nicht hab' Ist mir das Grab, Die ganze Welt Ist mir vergällt.	Every place is my grave When he isn't there My whole world Turns bitter.
Mein armer Kopf Ist mir verrückt, Mein armer Sinn Ist mir zerstückt.	My poor head Is crazy My poor mind Is all gone to pieces.
Meine Ruh' ist hin, Mein Herz ist schwer, Ich finde sie nimmer Und nimmermehr.	My heart's heavy I have lost my peace of mind And I'll never never Find it again.
Nach ihm nur schau' ich Zum Fenster hinaus, Nach ihm nur geh' ich Aus dem Haus.	It's only for him I look out the window, It's only to go to him I leave the house.
Sein hoher Gang, Sein' edle Gestalt, Seines Mundes Lächeln, Seiner Augen Gewalt,	His tall step His proud figure The smile on his mouth The power in his eyes.
Und seiner Rede Zauberfluß, Sein Händedruck, Und ach sein Kuß!	And his words Like a stream of magic The pressure of his hand, And oh, his kiss.
Meine Ruh' ist hin, Mein Herz ist schwer, Ich finde sie nimmer Und nimmermehr.	My heart's heavy I have lost my peace of mind And I'll never never Find it again.
Mein Busen drängt Sich nach ihm hin. Auch dürft' ich fassen Und halten ihn!	My bosom goes out To him in desire Oh, if only I could seize him And hold him
Und küssen ihn, So wie ich wollt', An seinen Küssen Vergehen sollt'!	And kiss him The way I want to, So I would die On his kisses.

**Gretchen im Zwinger
(Gretchens Bitte)**

Faust 1, ll.3587-3619.
*In der Mauerhöhle ein Andachtsbild der
Mater dolorosa, Blumenkrüge davor.*

Ach neige,
Du Schmerzenreiche,
Dein Antlitz gnädig meiner Not!

Das Schwert im Herzen,
Mit tausend Schmerzen
Blickst auf zu deines Sohnes Tod.

Zum Vater blickst du,

**Gretchen inside the town wall
(Gretchens Prayer)**

*In the niche of a wall a shrine, with an image of the
Mater Dolorosa. Pots of flowers before it*

Oh, you
who are full of sorrow
Incline your gracious face towards my affliction!

With a sword piercing your heart,
And a thousand griefs,
You gaze at your dead son

And raise your eyes to his Father,

Und Seufzer schickst du
Hinauf um sein' und deine Not.

And send up sighs
For his affliction and yours.

Wer fühlet,
Wie wühlet
Der Schmerz mir im Gebein?
Was mein armes Herz hier banget,
Was es zittert, was verlanget,
Weißt nur du, nur du allein!

Who can feel
How insidiously
The pain eats into my very bones?
What my poor heart dreads,
Why it trembles, what it desires,
Only you, only you can know!

Wohin ich immer gehe
Wie weh, wie weh, wie wehe
Wird mir im Busen hier!
Ich bin ach kaum alleine,
Ich wein', ich wein', ich weine,
Das Herz zerbricht in mir.

Wherever I go,
How it hurts, how it hurts
Here inside me!
Ah, as soon as I am alone,
I weep, I weep and weep,
And my heart inside me is breaking to pieces.

Die Scherben vor meinem Fenster
Betaut' ich mit Tränen, ach!
Als ich am frühen Morgen
Dir diese Blumen brach.

Oh my tears fell like dew
On the pots by my window
early this morning
When I picked these flowers for your shrine.

Schien hell in meine Kammer
Die Sonne früh herauf,
Saß ich in allem Jammer
In meinem Bett' schon auf.

When the bright sun shone
early into my room
I was sitting up in my bed already
In all my misery.

Hilf! Rette mich von Schmach und Tod!
Ach neige,
Du Schmerzenreiche,
Dein Antlitz gnädig meiner Not!

Help! Save me from disgrace and death!
Ah, you who are full of sorrow
Incline your gracious face
towards my affliction.

Szene aus Goethes *Faust*
Faust 1, ll. 3776-3834.

Scene from Goethe's *Faust*

Böser Geist:
Wie anders, Gretchen, war dir's,
Als du noch voll Unschuld
Hier zum Altar trat'st,
Aus dem vergriffnen Büchelchen
Gebete lalltest,
Halb Kinderspiele,
Halb Gott im Herzen!

The Evil Spirit:
How different things were for you, Gretchen
When you were still all innocence,
Approaching that altar,
Lisping prayers from your little
Worn prayer-book;
Your heart had nothing in it
But God and child's play!

Gretchen!
Wo steht dein Kopf?
In deinem Herzen,
Welche Missetat?
Bet'st du für deiner Mutter Seele,
Die durch dich zur langen,
Langen Pein hinüberschlief?
Auf deiner Schwelle wessen Blut?
– Und unter deinem Herzen
Regt sich's nicht quillend schon,
Und ängstet dich und sich
Mit ahndungsvoller Gegenwart?

Gretchen!
What are you thinking?
What misdeed
burdens your heart now?
Are you praying for your mother's soul,
Who by your doing
Overslept into long, long purgatorial pains?
Whose blood stains your doorstep?
- And under your heart is there not
Something stirring, welling up already,
A foreboding presence,
Feared by you and by itself?

Gretchen:
Weh! Weh!
Wär' ich der Gedanken los,
Die mir herüber und hinüber gehen

Gretchen:
Oh God! Oh God!
If I could get rid of these thoughts
That move across me and through me

Wider mich!	Against my will!

Chor:
Dies irae, dies illa,
Solvet saeclum in favilla,

The day of wrath, that day
Will dissolve the world in ashes,

Böser Geist:
Grimm faßt dich!
Die Posaune tönt!
Die Gräber beben!
Und dein Herz,
Aus Aschenruh'
Zu Flammenqualen
Wieder aufgeschaffen,
Bebt auf!

The Evil Spirit:
God's wrath seizes you!
The Last Trumpet scatters its sound!
The graves shudder open!
And your heart
That was at rest in its ashes
Is resurrected in fear,
fanned again to the flames
Of its torment!

Gretchen:
Wär' ich hier weg!
Mir ist als ob die Orgel mir
Den Atem versetzte,
Gesang mein Herz
Im Tiefsten lös'te.

Gretchen:
Let me get away from here!
It's as if the organ
Were choking me
And the singing melting
The heart deep down in me!

Chor:
Judex ergo cum sedebit,
Quidquid latet adparebit,
Nil inultum remanebit.

When therefore the judge will sit,
Whatever hides will appear:
Nothing will remain unpunished.

Gretchen:
Mir wird so eng!
Die Mauern-Pfeiler
Befangen mich!
Das Gewölbe
Drängt mich! – Luft!

Gretchen:
I can't breathe!
The great pillars
Are stifling me
The vaulted roof
Crushes me! – Give me air!

Böser Geist:
Verbirg' dich! Sünd' und Schande
Bleibt nicht verborgen,
Luft? Licht? Weh dir!

The Evil Spirit:
Hide yourself! Sin and shame
Cannot be hidden.
Air? Light? Woe on you!

Chor:
Quid sum miser tunc dicturus?
Quem patronum rogaturus?
Cum vix justus sit securus.

What will I say then in my wretchedness?
To whom do I turn for protection?

Böser Geist:
Ihr Antlitz wenden
Verklärte von dir ab.
Die Hände dir zu reichen,
Schauert's den Reinen.
Weh!

The Evil Spirit:
Souls in bliss
Have turned their faces from you.
They shrink from touching you,
For they are pure!
Woe!

Chor:
Quid sum miser tunc dicturus?
Quem patronum rogaturus?

Choir:
What will I say then in my wretchedness?
To whom do I turn for protection?

Gretchen:
Nachbarin! Euer Fläschchen! –

Gretchen:
Neighbour! Your smelling-salts!

(Sie fällt in Ohnmacht)

(She faints)

Gretchen's Song of Madness from the Kerkerszene (Prison Scene)

Faust 1, ll. 4412- 4420.

Meine Mutter, die Hur	Who killed me dead?
Die mich umgebracht hat!	My mother, the whore!
Mein Vater, der Schelm	Who ate my flesh?
Der mich gessen hat!	My father, for sure!
Mein Schwesterlein klein	Little sister gathered
Hub auf die Bein,	The bones he scattered;
An einem kühlen Ort;	In a cool, cool place they lie
Da ward ich ein schönes Waldvöglein,	And there I became a tiny bird so fine,
Fliege fort, fliege fort!	Fly away, fly away!

Translations: Lorraine Byrne Bodley

Printed by
CPI books GmbH, Leck